GEMS
OF
BIBLE DOCTRINE

GEMS
OF
BIBLE DOCTRINE

Denver Sizemore

College Press Publishing Company, Joplin, Missouri

Copyright © 1987
College Press Publishing Company

First Printing, June 1972
Second Printing, October 1978
Third Printing, April 1982
Fourth Printing, June 1987
Fifth Printing, June 1990

Printed and Bound in the
United States of America
All Rights Reserved

International Standard Book Number: 0-89900-218-8

TABLE OF CONTENTS

FORWARD

Denver Sizemore is Professor of New Testament at Atlanta Christian College, East Point, Georgia. He is a superlative teacher. The hours I spent in his classes are counted as some of the most valuable of my entire college career. But unlike many who sit in classrooms, Professor Sizemore is eminently practical. I doubt if any other one person in the state of Georgia has had any more influence upon the growth of the church than this man.

Professor Sizemore is a man of God. His advice is sought by students, preachers and officers in the churches. It is certainly obvious after a conversation with him that his foremost concern is the building of the kingdom of God.

His first volume of doctrinal studies, *Thirteen Lessons in Christian Doctrine*, was a real contribution to the literature of the Restoration Movement. The lessons were well outlined and aptly illustrated. We at the Englewood Christian Church, used them in our Bible School with great success. Many bought extra copies for their friends.

It is a privilege to write the Foreword for this second volume of studies. The topics chosen for consideration are timely. The lessons on the Holy Spirit should be especially helpful. I'm sure that the use of this study for one quarter in the Bible School curriculum will strengthen the church in many crucial areas.

Fred W. Smith, Jr.
Englewood Christian Church
Jacksonville, Florida

I

CHRISTIAN LOVE

I. The True Nature of Love.
  A. Four Greek words for love.
  B. The Meaning of Agape.
    1. Definitions.
    2. Agape is an act of the will.
    3. It is love for the undeserving.

II. The Elements of Love (Agape).

III. How to obtain this love.

IV. Some characteristics of Christian Love.
  A. Love manifests itself in action.
  B. Love is expressed in obedience to God.
  C. Love includes correction or reproof of sin.
  D. Agape—is love that cares.
  E. Love—Badge of identification for the Christian.
  F. Love is eternal and indestructible.

V. The challenge of love.

CHRISTIAN LOVE

Love has been called "the Great Dynamic." Paul calls it "the more excellent way" (I Cor. 12:31). Love is described as the greatest of the virtues; greater than faith or hope (I Cor. 13:13). In Galatians 5:22, love is presented as the "queen of the graces." Paul mentions love over 60 times in his epistles. The love of Christ is so great that it "passes (or surpasses) knowledge" (Eph. 3:19). "God is love" (I John 4:8) is the best description of God's character and nature to be found in the New Testament. Love lies at the very heart of Christianity and is essential to man's relations to God and to man (Matt. 22:37-39).

When the scribe asked Jesus what the greatest commandment was, He replied that the first is: "Thou shalt love the Lord they God with all thy heart, and with all thy soul, and with all thy mind, and with all thy strength. The second is this, Thou shalt love thy neighbor as thyself. There is none other commandment greater than these" (Mark 12:30-31). Jesus said that on these two commandments hang all the law and the prophets (Matt. 22:40). Paul states that love is the "fulfillment of the Law" (Rom. 13:8-10). All that the law and prophets contained had been distilled into this one command: "to love." When a person loves God, he will do everything that God commands and will abstain from the things that God condemns. If a person loves his neighbor "as himself" he will do nothing to hurt him, but do all he can to help him. This would fulfill God's law regarding both God and man.

I. THE TRUE NATURE OF LOVE

There is much talk of love today but often little understanding of its true nature.

"In our generation there is a lot of sticky sentimentality and trifling twaddle which parades as love. We use the word to describe our feelings for bicycles and Buicks, sandwiches and scenery, weather and wives. Thus the term has been washed out and squeezed dry of any transcendent quality. We need to study again the nature of a value so great that its essence is of God, a dynamic of such a vast potential that it is greater even than faith and hope."[1]

It is impossible to define love, just like it is impossible to define God. But, we can understand better what love is when we look at the elements of love and see how the word is used in the New Testament.

There are times when the English language, when compared

---

[1]Ketcherside, Carl, *Mission Messenger,* November 1969, p. 163.

with the Greek, is somewhat poverty-stricken. For example, in English, there is but one word for love and that word must do duty for many feelings and attitudes. But the Greek has four words:

A. Four Greek words for love.

1. Eros—This word is used primarily for love between the sexes. It is the love of a man for a maid. It has a predominant physical side and always involves sexual love.

This word does not appear in the New Testament. This is not because the New Testament rejects or degrades physical love but rather because by the time of Jesus this word had come to be connected with lust rather than with love in its higher sense. Eros has been called "love still unconverted."

2. Philia—This word describes the warm, intimate, personal affection one holds toward friends and relatives. It may include some of the physical side of love but it includes much more. Philia is the more comprehensive word for love and includes every degree and kind of love or liking. God is said to have this kind of love for Jesus (John 5:20). He also has this kind of love for Jesus's disciples (John 16:27). It describes God's warm personal feelings toward those who love Him.

3. storge—This word is not found in the New Testament but is used in secular Greek writings. This word is limited to family love, such as the love of parents for their children or children for their parents.

4. Agape—This is the word that is mostly used when speaking of love in its true Christian sense. This word is rarely used in secular Greek but is used abundantly in the New Testament. R.C. Trench wrote, "Agape is a word born within the bosom of revealed religion." This word with its full meaning is distinctly a Christian word. This is not accidental. Agape is a new word to describe new ideas, new qualities of life. It describes a new attitude to others; an attitude born within the Christian fellowship and describes love that is impossible without the Christian dynamic.

B. The meaning of Agape.

1. Definitions. Frederick D. Kershner defined agape as "intelligent good will."

William Barclay defines it as "unconquerable benevolence, undefeatable goodwill." Agape is the spirit in the heart which will never seek anything but the highest good for its fellow men.

Carl Ketcherside describes love as that "active and beneficent good will which stops at nothing to achieve the good of the beloved object."[1]

2. *This (agape) love is not an emotion or sentiment but an act of the will.* By definition this love is an intelligent, goodwill toward the object of its love. One loves by a deliberate choice. It is an action of the mind and the will, not just the emotions.

In Matthew 5:43-48 God is pictured as deliberately making his sun to rise on the evil and the good. He sends rain on the just and the unjust. This is a result of God's decision to love all men regardless of their worthiness or reaction to Him.

For this reason agape love can be commanded. Jesus said, "a new commandment I give unto you, that ye love one another" (John 13:34). One cannot command emotions. Emotions cannot always be controlled or directed. But, since this love is primarily an act of the will and the mind, it can be commanded This is the word that Jesus used in Matthew 5:44-46 when he commanded the disciples to "love your enemies." Three times Jesus used the word agape when he gave this command. Many people misunderstand this command because they think that Jesus is requiring the same emotional attachment toward one's enemies as to close friends or brothers in Christ. Professor R.C. Foster in commenting on Jesus' statement writes, "We are commanded to forgive and to hold a kindly feeling toward those who hate us, to salute them, pray for them, do good to them as opportunity offers, but we are not commanded to make intimate, personal associates of them."[1]

3. *It is love for the unworthy and undeserving.* The Greek philosopher Aristotle held that a man cannot expect to be loved unless he is deserving of love. His whole attitude seemed to be that if there is nothing in a person to arouse affection then he should not expect to be loved. Human love is usually a re-

---

[1]Ketcherside, Carl, *Mission Messenger*, November 1969, p. 164.
[1]Foster, R.C., *The Final Week*, (Baker Book House, 1962), p. 289.

sponse to something worthy or lovable in the other person. This
s the big difference between purely human love and agape or
divine love. Agape is the love of the completely unworthy. Paul
writes: "But God commendeth his love toward us, in that, while
we were yet sinners, Christ died for us" (Rom. 5:6-8). God loves
not because man is worthy or is lovable but because it is the very
nature of God to love. God loves us because we need it not
because we deserve it.

II. THE ELEMENTS OF LOVE

In the "Psalm of Love" (I Cor. 13), Paul describes the
elements of divine love. He takes this heavenly ray of light and
passes it through the magnificent prism of his mind and breaks
it down into its component parts.

In I Corinthians 13:4-7, Paul lists fifteen characteristics of
love. Upon examination we find that love is composed of simple,
basic virtues of Christian living. When put together they form
the wonderful grace of love. If one would have love in his life he
must exhibit these virtues. Paul presents these elements of love
by listing two positive qualities, then eight negative qualities and
then concludes with five positive qualities of love. Let us examine
a few of these.

A. *Love is patient*—"suffereth long." The Greek word
points to patience with people rather than with circumstances.
Origen said this word was used of a man who is wronged and
who has it in his power to avenge himself and yet does not. This
speaks eloquently of love's self-restraint. In Ephesians 4:1-2 Paul
writes: "I . . . beseech you to walk worthily of the Lord where-
with ye were called, with all lowliness and meekness, with longsuffering, forbearing one another in love"—(AMP—or "bearing one another and making allowances because you love one
another"). Love is patient! God is patient.

"The baby helped snap beans today;
She saved the bad, threw good away.
I thought how patient God must be,
When I help him as she helped me."

B. *Kind*—Paired with this more passive side of love is a

5

corresponding active side—kindness. Paul writes "be kind one to another, tenderhearted, forgiving each other . . ." (Eph. 4:32). Kindness endeavors to sweeten and bless those about it and shrinks from giving pain. The idea is that under all provocations and ill-usage it is gentle and mild. Kindness was a chief characteristic of Jesus' ministry.

C. *Envieth not*—Knows no envy or jealousy. Envy is a serious sin. "A tranquil heart is the life of the flesh; but envy is the rottenness of the bones" (Prov. 14:30).

It was envy that caused Joseph's brothers to sell him into slavery. Envy caused King Saul to hate and try to destroy David. Love preserves one from envying others who may be greater or richer or better than himself. The ability to rejoice with others in their good fortunes is perhaps the best test of a man's character. We do not envy when we love.

D. *Vaunteth not itself*—Not arrogant or boastful. The root meaning of the word boastful is "windbag." Behind boastful bragging there usually lies conceit and an over estimation of ones' own importance or abilities. Love is not conceited. Love is concerned with giving of itself rather than asserting itself in foolish pride. Jesus said "everyone that exalteth himself shall be humbled; and he that humbleth himself shall be exalted" (Luke 14:11).

E. *Seeketh not her own*—It does not insist upon its rights. There are two kinds of people in the world: those who continually think of their rights and those who continually think of their duties. The first type thinks of what life owes them but the other thinks of what they owe to life. We see this quality in our Lord. "For ye know the grace of our Lord Jesus Christ, that though he was rich, yet for your sakes he became poor, that ye through his poverty might become rich" (II Cor. 8:9). Love is unselfish.

F. *Not easily provoked and takes no account of evil*—Here are two elements of love. The first indicates that one who is controlled by love is not irritable or touchy and does not take offense readily. Paul's life was full of abuse, insult, and injury, yet he urged the Romans to feed their enemies if they were hungry and give them drink if they were thirsty. This was so the

6

Christians would not be overcome with evil but rather would overcome evil with good (Rom. 12:20-21).

The second element means not "resentful." This is an accountant's word which means to enter an item in a ledger so that it will not be forgotten. The Christian does not store in his memory every wrong he has received. This will soon gender resentment and hate. Love has learned the great lesson of forgetting. Chrysostom wrote, "as a spark falls into the sea and does not harm the sea, so harm may be done to a loving soul and is soon quenched without disturbing the soul."[1] These are a few of the elements of love. God has this love for man and wants man to have it for Him and for each other.

III. HOW TO OBTAIN THIS LOVE

Agape is a divine love and the Scriptures teach that it can come only from God. Paul writes: "Because the love of God hath been shed abroad in our hearts through the Holy Spirit which was given unto us" (Rom. 5:5). Paul attributes to the Holy Spirit the presence of love in our hearts.

In Galatians 5:22 love is called the "fruit of the spirit." It is a fruit of righteousness produced in our lives by the power of the Holy Spirit. John writes, "We love, because he first loved us" (I John 4:19). Some translations read, "We love Him", but the word Him is not found in the better manuscripts. The idea is that we are enabled to love because God first loved us. "His love transforms us, dries up the fountain of selfishness within, and makes us capable of loving through the indwelling Spirit."[2] We are *capable* of loving only because we are first the *object* of this love.

IV. SOME CHARACTERISTICS OF CHRISTIAN LOVE

A. *Love manifests itself in action.* It is an old axiom that one may do without loving but that it is impossible to love without doing. Love naturally seeks expression toward the object

---

[1]Lenski, R.C.H., *The Interpretation of St. Paul's First and Second Epistle to the Corinthians*, (Wartburg Press, 1937), p. 558.

[2]Ketcherside, Carl, *Mission Messenger*, November 1969, p. 163.

of its love. "Herein was the love of God manifested in us, that God hath sent his only begotten son into the world that we might live through Him" (I John 4:9). The proof of God's love was revealed to man when He sent Jesus to earth (John 3:16). The apostle John exhorts the early Christians "let us not love in word, neither with the tongue; but in deed and truth" (I John 3:18). Love can be expressed in words but not in words alone. Love is best seen when it is demonstrated by action.

B. *Love is expressed in obedience to God and Christ.* Jesus said, "If ye love me, ye will keep my commandments" (John 14:15). Jesus told his apostles, "Not every one that saith unto me, Lord, Lord, shall enter into the kingdom of heaven; but he that doeth the will of my Father who is in heaven" (Matt. 7:21). He continued by saying, "Why do you keep calling me Lord, Lord and never do what I tell you?" (Luke 6:46-NEB). Love is shown in obedience to God.

C. *Love includes correction or reproof of sin.* God's love is expressed to His children through his chastening. "My son, regard not lightly the chastening of the Lord, nor faint when thou art reproved of him; For whom the Lord loveth he chasteneth, and scourgeth every son whom he receiveth" (Heb. 12:5-6). God's love may be better seen in his chastening than in his blessings. When a parent punishes a child for darting into a busy street he does it to save the child's life. This is love.

By the same token Christians are to help one another. This often includes reproving, rebuking, and exhorting (II Tim. 4:2). This is done in love for the purpose of restoring and helping the sinning one to get back on the right path with God. It should be done gently and humbly but love requires the stronger to help the weak in the spiritual life (Gal. 6:1).

D. *Agape is love that cares.* The ancient philosophers had one aim in life: to seek peace of mind—serenity for the soul. In order to attain this, the pagans taught the utter necessity of two basic qualities: first, the necessity of self-sufficiency. Self-sufficiency is the absolute independence of anything or anyone outside one's self. They sought to find peace entirely within themselves. The second basic quality was a complete indifference to joy or sorrow, gladness or grief. The heart was to be insulated from all feeling and emotion. They sought this attitude of mind so that nothing would affect them or disturb their calm.

If this is the goal of life then it is easy to see that the great enemy of peace is love. Love is the great disturber. Epictetus insisted that men should never set their hearts on anyone or anything. He taught that a man must teach himself not to care.

In direct contrast to this, agape, or Christian love is *caring*. The pagan philosophers said, "teach yourself not to care lest you be hurt." The Christian message says, "teach yourselves to care intensely for men, even though it does hurt." God cared so much that it cost him His son (John 3:16). Paul writes "rejoice with them that rejoice; weep with them that weep" (Rom. 12:15). This caring is obvious on every page of the New Testament. There is a high cost of loving. Jesus cared and it cost him his life. The Good Samaritan cared and it cost him effort, time, and money. The apostle Paul loved and cared and in II Corinthians 11 he describes the high cost of that love. He concludes the long list of sufferings with these words, "besides those things that are without, there is that which presseth upon me daily, anxiety for all the churches. Who is weak and I am not weak? Who is caused to stumble and I burn not?" (II Cor. 11:28-29). Despite the high cost the way of love is still the happiest and best way. How thankful we are that God loved and cared for us.

E. *Love is the badge of identification for the Christian.* Jesus told his disciples, "By this shall all men know that ye are my disciples, if ye have love one to another" (John 13:35). The apostle John echoes the Master's words when he says, "If a man say, I love God, and hateth his brother, he is a liar; for he that loveth not his brother whom he hath seen, cannot love God whom he hath not seen" (I John 4:20).

Jesus further exhorted his disciples to "love your enemies, and pray for them that persecute you; that ye may be sons of your Father who is in heaven" (Matt. 5:44-45). Love is a sure indication that one has passed from death into life. "We know that we have passed out of death into life, because we love the brethren. He that loveth not abideth in death" (I John 3:14). Love identifies the disciple as belonging to God, who is love.

F. *Love is eternal and indestructible.* "Love knows no

limit to its endurance, no end to its trust, no fading of its hope; it can outlast anything. It is, in fact, the one thing that still stands when all else has fallen" (I Cor. 13:7—Phillips Translation).

V. THE CHALLENGE OF LOVE

When man faces the fact that God loves him and has proved it in practical terms, he is faced with a challenge—a decision. He cannot simply ignore it; he must either return this love or else reject it. When a man loves a woman and gives her every evidence of it, she is faced with a decision. She cannot simply ignore it; she must either return his love or reject it. The same is true of the love of God. Herein lies man's condemnation. When he spurns the love of God, he not only hurts God but shuts himself up to a loveless life away from God. Jude's exhortation is a fitting one for this lesson when he said, "Keep yourselves in the love of God, looking for the mercy of our Lord Jesus Christ unto eternal life" (Jude 21).

"Were the whole realm of nature mine,
That were a present far too small;
Love so amazing, so Divine,
Demands my soul, my life, my all."

REVIEW QUESTIONS — LOVE

FILL IN THE BLANKS

1. List three facts showing the importance of Love.

    a. _____

    b. _____

    c. _____

2. Give a brief definition of the four words for love.

    a. _____

    b. _____

    c. _____

    d. _____

3. Why can agape—love be commanded? _____

_____.

4. Which love are we to have for our enemies? _____.

5. List three characteristics of love:

a. _____

b. _____

c. _____

6. What challenge does God's love present to man? _____

_____.

II

SIN

I. The Origin of Sin.

II. What is Sin?
  A. Words Translated Sin.
    1. Sin is lawlessness.
    2. Sin is transgression of God's laws.
    3. Sin is missing the mark.
  B. Failure to do right—omission.

III. Characteristics of Sin.
  A. Sin is selfish.
  B. It allures.
  C. It deceives.
  D. It enslaves.

IV. Consequences of Sin.
  A. Sin separates from God.
  B. Sin takes peace from the soul.
  C. Sin brings suffering.
  D. Sin brings death.

V. Cure for Sin.
  A. Jesus Himself provided the cure through His Sacrifice on the Cross.
  B. His blood cleanses from sin.
  C. Obedience to the gospel is necessary to the cure.

SIN

Dr. J.H. Jowett once said, "I covet no phraseology that

lends respectability to sin. The sorest injury we can do a man is to lighten his conception of the enormity of sin." R.G. Lee writes, "Sin is the most heinous and hellish thing in God's universe."[1]

I. THE ORIGIN OF SIN

Sin originated in the Garden of Eden when Eve, deceived by the serpent, ate the forbidden fruit. Adam was not deceived but he ate the fruit anyway. Man became a sinner by hearing, believing and obeying a lie, preached by the devil himself through the serpent (Gen. 3:1-8).

This act of disobedience brought sin into the world. Sin in turn brought death, for God had said "in the day that thou eatest thereof, thou shalt surely die" (Gen. 2:17b). In this act, Adam and Eve lost their pure, holy characters. They lost a beautiful home in the Garden of Eden. They lost the immediate presence of God, and eventually lost their physical lives. Thus, the evil trail of sin began to wind its wicked way through the history of man. Sin is universal. Christ is the only exception (Rom. 3:23; I Peter 2:22).

II. WHAT IS SIN?

In answering the question "What is sin?", let us look at the Greek words that are translated sin. Their meanings will be helpful in understanding sin.

A. *Words translated sin.*

1. Sin is lawlessness. The Greek word "anomia" means "to break or violate God's law." It is an opposition to and a disregard of a law of God. "Everyone that doeth sin doeth also lawlessness; and sin is lawlessness" (I John 3:4).

This is illustrated in the actions of Adam and Eve. Some have sneeringly asked, "Why suspend the destiny of the world on so trivial a circumstance as the eating of an apple?" Two things are wrong in this question. First, the Bible does not say it was an apple, it simply refers to it as "fruit" (Gen. 3:3). Second-

---

[1]Lee, R.G., *How To Lead a Soul to Christ*, (Zondervan Publishing House), p. 7-8.

13

ly, the eating of the forbidden fruit was not a trivial matter. This statement is made out of ignorance concerning the purpose of God's prohibition and the gravity of the act of Adam and Eve. God's purpose in the forbidden tree was twofold:

(a) *self-control*—Man was created with a free will. Could he use this free will in a mature way? Could man exercise self-control in its use? This is the first test of man's use of this new freedom and power.

(b) *loyalty to God*—Every human government has some test to determine loyalty and disloyalty. No fairer or better test of man's loyalty could God have given. First, it was simple and easily understood. There was only one tree forbidden. The command was clear, "thou shalt not eat." No rational being could have mistaken what was required by this command. Second, it was designed so that any disobedience would proceed from a spirit of disloyalty or rebellion. Like all positive commands, it would depend solely on the love of man for God and the spirit of obedience to God. For example, there did not seem to be, rationally speaking, any good reason why Adam and Eve should not eat of this tree. It was beautiful to look at, it was good for food, and it would make one wise. The real reason for not eating then would be respect for God's Word when He forbade it. Likewise, if they did eat, it was a clear case of disobedience to God's Word.

This test of loyalty was not the cause of their disloyalty; it was simply the occasion and proof of it. Adam and Eve had rebelled against God in their hearts; eating the fruit simply revealed this rebellion. This is the essence of all sin and consequently, illustrates the real evil of sin.

2. Sin is a transgression of God's law. The Greek word "paralthon" means an "overstepping of the law" of God; a disregard for the divine boundary between right and wrong. It is a violation of another's domain—God's law. The elder son in the parable of the Prodigal Son uses this word when he tells the father that he has never transgressed one of his commands (Luke 15:29).

David described his sin with Bathsheba as a transgression

when he prayed to God to have mercy upon him and "blot out my transgressions" (Psalms 51:1).

3. Sin is "missing the mark." The word "hamartia" means "missing the mark" or failing to meet the divine standard of perfection—God's target. Paul illustrates this in Romans 3:23 when he says, "For all have sinned, and fall short of the glory of God." All men do at some time sin and fall short of fulfilling their divine purpose in the world of glorifying God (Isa. 43:7; I Cor. 6:20; I Pet. 2:9). The arrow does not reach the mark. Man in his efforts to live righteously fails to reach it and therefore, like the arrow, falls short or goes wide of the mark—perfection. This is called sin.

These words describe sins of commission, where one actually breaks a command of God.

B. *Failure to do right—Omission.* One may also sin by being indifferent to God's commands. James wrote: "to him therefore that knoweth to do good (right) and doeth it *not* to him it is sin" (James 4:17). Neglecting to do that which is right, or being indifferent and unconcerned where God has spoken is sin. In the Parable of the Sheep and the Goats, those on the "goat" side were guilty of this type of sin (Matt. 25:31-46). For other illustrations see Matthew 25:14-30; Luke 16:19-31.

III. CHARACTERISTICS OF SIN

A. *Sin is selfish.* The essential principle of sin is selfishness. The chief characteristic of love (divine love) is giving—giving of itself and all it possesses to the object of its love. Sin is just the opposite. It is getting something for itself regardless of the cost and hurt to others.

"There never was a sin committed that was not the choice of self in preference to God. Every appeal that Satan made to the Saviour, on the mount of temptation, was an appeal to self: first, to *self-satisfaction*, or to satisfy His physical self which hungered; second, to *self pride*, or a suggestion that He appear in a miraculous demonstration, rather than by way of the Cross; and the third, an appeal to *self-aggrandizement*, offering Him all

15

the kingdoms of this world if He would but fall down and worship the Tempter. It is significant that the only weapon which the Master used to defeat these subtle suggestions was the Word of God, the revelation of *God's will*. His reply, in every case, was "It is written," etc. (Matt. 4:1-11). *Sin is the choice of self above God.*"[1]

B. *It allures*. Sin has the power to charm, to fascinate, to allure. This is why it is a temptation—it does appeal to man.

Sin has pleasure in it. Moses had to make a choice between sharing suffering and ill-treatment with the people of God or "to enjoy the pleasures of sin for a season" (Heb. 11:25). Granted, the pleasure of sin is short-lived, a fleeting pleasure, but still it is alluring and attracting.

The serpent approached Eve with a threefold appeal: (1) he appealed to the desires of the flesh by pointing out that the fruit was good to eat. (2) He appealed to her sense of beauty or "lust of the eyes" by calling to her attention that it was a delight to the eyes. (3) He appealed to her ambition or pride by suggesting that it would make her wise like God. John states that there are three types of temptation or lust in the world: "the lust of the flesh, and the lust of the eyes, and the vainglory (pride) of life" (I John 2:16). Eve was subjected to all three of these alluring temptations. Sin still makes its deceptive appeal to man along these same three lines of temptation.

Like the candle fly that is irresistibly drawn to the glittering flame only to be burned to death, man is often allured by the enticements of sin to his own destruction.

C. *It deceives*. Sin exhibits its pleasures but conceals its pain and shame. Sin promises more and gives less than anything known to man. The serpent pointed out all the seeming advantages to Eve, but covered the awful penalty and suffering with a mask. Hebrews 3:13 says "exhort one another day by day, so long as it is called Today; lest any one of you be hardened by the deceitfulness of sin." Satan would have us think of sin as a thing of beauty, pleasure, and innocence. Like the rainbow over

---

[1]Crawford, C.C., *Sermon Outlines on the Cross of Christ*, p. 21.

the cataract, he strives to hide the destruction and death of sin under a halo of pleasure. Liquor ads are a good illustration of this. They portray the pleasure but never the "finished product" of this evil trade. Satan pictures sin the same way.

D. *It enslaves.* Sin deceptively offers freedom and liberation from the unpleasantness and drudgery of life. But instead it gives a chain of slavery to sin. Paul says in Romans 6:16, "Know ye not, that to whom ye present your selves as servants unto obedience, his servants ye are whom ye obey; whether of sin unto death, or of obedience unto righteousness?"

The Prodigal Son was lured by the charm of those "faraway places," with its freedom from his father's control. Sin, however, paid him off in rags, bare feet, hunger, and toil in a hog pen. Sin paralyzes the will, corrupts the affections, blinds the intellect, and enslaves the soul. Paul urges Timothy to patiently teach in order that those who have fallen into sin may recover themselves or return to their senses "out of the snare of the devil, having been taken captive by him unto his will" (II Tim. 2:26).

Samson, the free-frolicking young giant who refused to take sin seriously, ended up in the Philistine mill, blind and powerless, grinding their grain. This is a picture of the enslaving power of sin.

IV. CONSEQUENCES OF SIN

A. *Sin separates from God.* Isaiah told Israel: "Behold, Jehovah's hand is not shortened, that it cannot save; neither his ear heavy, that it cannot hear: but your iniquities have separated between you and your God, and your sins have hid his face from you, so that he will not hear" (Isa. 59:1-2). Before sin entered the Garden of Eden, God would come down in the cool of the day and talk with his children. Here was holy fellowship between God and man. Sin changed that.

When sin entered their lives God, because of his holy nature, could not associate with them directly. They were driven from His presence and the angel with the flaming sword prevented their return. God continued to bless and provide for them, but they had lost the close association He had with them before sin marred their lives. Sin, if persisted in, will separate us from God both in this life and in that which is to come.

    B. *Sin takes peace from the soul.* "There is no peace. saith Jehovah, to the wicked" (Isa. 48:22). David said after his sin with Bathsheba. "I know my transgressions; and my sin is ever before me" (Psalms 51:4). Judas was miserable after he betrayed the Master. No doubt he wandered the streets of Jerusalem all night afraid to meet the other apostles, tormented by his own conscience until finally in a desperate effort o relieve the guilt of his soul, he rushed up the hill to the temple declaring "I have sinned in that I betrayed innocent blood" (Matt. 27:3). Speaking of the wicked, Paul says, "The way of peace have they not known" (Rom. 3:17).

There is the classic example of the French King. Against his wishes, in a weak hour, he had been persuaded to sign a decree, legalizing the murder of the Huguenots. The assassination was to take place on St. Bartholomew's eve. It was to be signalized by the ringing of the church bells. The hour came for the black murder and simultaneously the bells of Notre Dame and the other great cathedrals broke into a fury of clanging sounds. The murders leaped to their throat-slitting and the streets of Paris ran red with blood. Well, time has its great avengings. The king is dying. Is not his couch soft? Shall he not find a pleasant passing? What says history? Half-starting from his pillow, even in the moment of death's agony, "Don't you hear them, the bells, the bells?" and sank back on his pillow, dead.

Only the Prince of Peace as He forgives sin can bring the peace that passes understanding.

"In vain I seek for rest In all created good;
It leaves me yet unblest, And makes me pant for God.
And sure at rest I cannot be Until my heart find rest in thee."

    C. *Sin brings suffering.* Sin brought suffering to Eve through the pain of bearing children (Gen. 3:16). Sin brought suffering to Adam as he toiled to provide a living for his family

18

(Gen. 3:19). The earth suffered from the curse placed upon it (Gen. 3:18; cf. Rom. 8:19-22). Finally, the serpent was also made to suffer for his part in the fall of man (Gen. 3:14-15). Everyone and everything suffered when sin entered the world.

Someone has said that "the history of our race is that of a funeral march from the cradle to the grave, to the music of the widow's sigh and the orphan's cry. If all the tears shed from first to last were gathered into one volume, they would make a new ocean deeper than the Atlantic and broader than the Pacific. Were all the groans uttered from the beginning till now gathered into one volume of sound, there would be a peal of thunder louder than ever crashed the mountains of the sky. Were all broken hearts from Eden to Gethsemane, and thence on to the present time, gathered together, there would be a new mountain range vaster than the Andes and higher than the Himalayas."

D. *Sin brings death.* The penalty for sin is death. "Wherefore, as by one man sin entered into the world and death by sin; and so death passed upon all men, for that all have sinned" (Rom. 5:12, KJV). Ezekiel adds, "the soul that sinneth it shall die" (Ezek. 18:4b).

Sin brings two types of death. First it brings physical death. Because of the perfect body God had given Adam, it took death 930 years to destroy it (Gen. 5:5). Yet it did. Every cemetery today is a silent reminder that the penalty for sin is death. Secondly, sin brings spiritual death. Paul reminded the Thessalonian Christians that when Christ returns, those who know not God and who obey not the gospel of Jesus "shall be punished with everlasting destruction (banishment) from the presence of the Lord, and from the glory of his power" (II Thess. 1:9, KJV). Separation from God is spiritual death.

V. CURE FOR SIN

In the face of overwhelming sin on every hand, man is tempted to cry out with Jeremiah, "Is there no balm in Gilead, is there no physician there?" (Jer. 8:22).

19

Yes there is a balm in Gilead and Jesus the great physician stands ready to administer it to anyone who will call on Him. God spoke to Israel and said, "Come now, and let us reason together, saith Jehovah: though your sins be as scarlet, they shall be as white as snow; though they be red like crimson, they shall be as wool" (Isa. 1:18). Sinners in the New Testament were told to "repent ye therefore, and turn again, that your sins may be blotted out" (Acts 3:19).

A. *Jesus himself provided the cure through His sacrifice on the cross.* Peter writes, "who his own self bare our sins in his body upon the tree, that we, having died unto sins, might live unto righteousness; by whose stripes ye were healed" (I Peter 2:24). Paul says that "Christ died for our sins" (I Cor. 15:3). Again Paul declares that our salvation "hath now been manifested by the appearing of our Saviour Christ Jesus, who abolished death, and brought life and immortality to light through the gospel" (II Tim. 1:10).

B. *His blood cleanses from sin.* Through Christ "we have our redemption through His blood, the forgiveness of our trespasses, according to the riches of his grace" (Eph. 1:7; cf. Rom. 3:25). Peter confirms this when he says "Ye were redeemed, not with corruptible things, with silver or gold, from your vain manner of life handed down from your fathers; but with precious blood, as of a lamb without blemish and without spot, even the blood of Christ" (I Peter 1:18-19); cf. I John 1:7; Rev. 1:5).

C. *Obedience to the gospel is necessary to obtain the cure.* To the broken hearted sinners on Pentecost who cried out, "what shall we do?" Peter said, "Repent ye, and be baptized every one of you in the name of Jesus Christ unto the remission of your sins; and ye shall receive the gift of the Holy Spirit" (Acts 2:38; cf. Mark 16:16).

Our part in God's plan for removing sin is *faith* in Christ, which changes the mind from indifference to trust, thus destroying the love of sin; *repentance* that changes the will, and destroys the practice of sin; *baptism* into Christ that changes the relationship from a believer out of Christ to one *in* Christ, thus destroying the state of sin. Through this obedience we are brought into contact with the blood of Christ, which cleanses us from all sin.

"What can wash away my sin?
Nothing but the blood of Jesus;
What can make me whole again?
Nothing but the blood of Jesus."

REVIEW QUESTIONS — SIN

Fill in the Blanks:

1. Man became a sinner by _____, _____, and _____ a lie (Gen. 3:1-8).

2. Through disobedience Adam and Eve lost: (1) _____ (2) _____, (3) _____ and (4) _____.

3. List three definitions of sin: (1) _____ (2) _____, and (3) _____.

4. What was God's purpose in the forbidden Tree? _____

5. List three characteristics of sin: (1) _____ (2) _____, and (3) _____.

6. What obedience is required to obtain the cure for sin? _____

III

SATAN

I. Names for Satan.
   A. Satan.
   B. Devil
   C. Other titles or epithets for the Devil.

II. Origin and History of Satan.
   A. Origin of Satan.
   B. His role in the fall of man.
   C. Gradual revealing of Satan.

III. His character.
   A. He is a liar.
   B. He is a murderer.
   C. He is deceitful.
   D. He is malicious.

IV. His Work.
   A. He is a ruler of a powerful and evil kingdom.
   B. His work as tempter.

V. Satan can be resisted.
   A. God has limited his powers of temptation.
   B. Satan must be resisted.

VI. Destiny of Satan.
   A. Christ came to destroy the works of Satan.
   B. The Lake of Fire is his destiny.

SATAN

Evil is in the world. It is here because of man's disobedience to the laws of God. However, the Bible teaches that man has had help in producing this plague of sin that pervades the world. The

Bible identifies this evil one as Satan, or the devil. This evil being is the adversary of both God and man. This lesson is written that the reader may be aware of his "devices", "Lest Satan should get an advantage of us" (II Cor. 2:11).

I. NAMES FOR SATAN

A. *Satan*. This word, which is a transliteration of the Hebrew word, "Satan" means "adversary or opponent". The Greek word for Satan in the New Testament, *Satanas*, is also translated "adversary," or "one who opposes" like in a court of law. Satan was such an opponent to Job, when He did his best to persuade God to let him destroy Job (Job 1-2). Peter reminds us that Satan stalks the Christian like a lion eager to devour its prey (I Peter 5:8).

B. *Devil*. This word used mostly in the New Testament is the Greek word "diabolos", which means "slanderer or accuser". Because of his hatred of all that is good, Satan slanders both God and man. (1) In the Garden of Eden he slandered God affirming that God had lied when he told Adam and Eve that if they ate the forbidden fruit they would die (Gen. 3:1-5). (2) In the case of Job, Satan slandered man to God, when he accused Job of serving God merely for financial gain (Job 1:9-11; cf., Rev. 12:10). Both of these names designate a personal evil being.

The term "devils" found in the King James Version should be translated "demons." There are many demons but only one devil.

C. *Other titles or epithets for the devil.* Many conservative scholars hold that the word Lucifer in Isaiah 14:12-14 (translated "day star" in ASV) refers to Satan. They also believe that the anointed cherub mentioned in Ezekiel 28:12-15 refers to Satan.

Many other scholars, however, contend that these passages refer to the kings of Babylon and Tyre respectively. Isaiah 14:4 states that this passage is a "proverb or parable," against the King of Babylon. It seems clear that Isaiah 14:12-14 is primarily a denunciation of the King of Babylon.

Other titles or epithets describing Satan's character and work are these: Abaddon, or Apollyon, (Rev. 9:11); "accuser of

23

the brethren" (Rev. 2:10); Beelzebub (Matt. 12:24); Belial (II Cor. 6:15); "deceiver of the whole world" (Rev. 12:9); "the great dragon" (Rev. 12:9); "evil one" (Matt. 13:19, 38; I John 2:13, 5:19); "father of lies" (John 8:44); "a murderer" (John 8:44); "the old serpent" (Rev. 12:9); and "the tempter" (Matt. 4:5; I Thess. 3:5).

II. ORIGIN AND HISTORY OF SATAN

A. *Origin of Satan.* The origin of Satan is not clearly stated in the scriptures. In Revelation 20:1 Satan is referred to as the "angel" of the "abyss". He is called a King whose name is Apollyon which means "destroyer" (Rev. 9:11).

The Bible speaks of angels who sinned because they kept not their first estate or domain of responsibilities and left their proper home, or habitation. These are said to be reserved in everlasting chains until judgment (Jude 6). Peter adds that these fallen angels were cast down to hell (Greek—"tartarus") and kept in pits of darkness until the judgment (II Peter 2:4). Some have concluded from these statements that Satan was the leader of these angels or of a group like them, who rebelled against God and were evicted from Heaven. Jesus said that Satan abode not in the truth (John 8:44), implying that he is a fallen being. Paul indicates that Satan fell under God's condemnation because of ambitious pride (I Tim. 3:6). If Revelation 12:7-9 in any way refers to Satan's fall then it would seem that he was a personage of some rank in heaven and that he had many associates in his rebellion. It states that the devil "was cast down to the earth, and, angels were cast down with him" (Rev. 12:9b). Jesus also spoke of the devil and his angels (Matt. 25:41). All these references point to the conclusion that Satan was a high creature of prominence in Heaven who lead a rebellion and was thrown out.

His opposition to God has continued on earth. His plan seems to be to win the allegiance of man to himself and away from God. This will be apparent as we continue this study.

The obvious question is, "If God created Satan, how did he become evil?" The answer seems to lie in the area of his free will to choose good or evil. Man was created perfect and then taking the gift of choice used it against God and thus became sinful.

24

This seems to be the answer as to how Satan and the angels though created good, became evil.

B. *Satan's role in the fall of man.* Satan's name is not mentioned in connection with the fall of man in the Garden of Eden. The Genesis account attributes the temptations to the serpent—Hebrew—"the hisser" (Gen. 3:1-5). The serpent was said to be more subtle than any beast of the field. His cleverness is seen in his approach to Eve. He is definitely her superior in reasoning and persuasion. If the serpent was acting alone, this was inconsistent with the fact that man had been given the dominion over all things (Gen. 1:28). Here was a creature greater than man. This leads one to the conclusion that the serpent was given this wisdom and power to speak and reason by a superior being. If God could empower Baalam's ass to speak, could not Satan use the serpent in a similar way?

Other reasons why the Bible points to Satan as the real culpit are these:

1. Satan is called the father of liars. "He was a murderer from the beginning, and standeth not in the truth, because there is no truth in him. When he speaketh a lie, he speaketh of his own: for he is a liar, and the father thereof" (John 8:44). The serpent told Eve the first falsehood that was uttered on earth. The source of the lie was Satan its "Father".

2. Satan is called the first murderer. "He was a murderer *from the beginning*" (John 8:44). In the Garden of Eden death was brought upon mankind through the deception and disobedience of Eve. If Satan fabricated the lie that led to death then he is the real murderer and the first one.

3. A third reason why Satan was the real tempter of our first parents is that he is called "the old serpent" in the New Testament (Rev. 12:9; 20:4). This seems to allude to the incident in Eden. The diabolical cunning and malice exhibited by the serpent certainly seems to fit Satan as he is portrayed in the Bible.

C. *Satan gradually revealed in the Bible.* Satan is mentioned only a few times in the Old Testament. The full unveiling of Satan as a powerful, evil ruler is reserved for the New Testament.

In the Old Testament Satan is still permitted to be in the

presence of God even though he has fallen from God's favor. For example, in Job 1:6 it is stated, "Now it came to pass on the day when the sons of God came to present themselves before Jehovah, that Satan also came among them." His evil nature, however, is obvious in his slandering of Job before God. In I Chronicles 21:1, Satan is said to have stood up against Israel and moved David to number Israel, which brought on God's wrath and the destructive plague. In Zechariah 3:1 Satan is pictured as resisting Joshua, the high priest. Undoubtedly, Satan was the moving spirit behind most of the evil in the Old Testament but his role is not clearly revealed at that time.

In the New Testament his character and evil works are clearly delineated. The two terms Satan and Devil are mentioned over one hundred times in the New Testament. He is the tempter of all men including the Lord Jesus Christ (Matt. 4). He is in violent conflict with the followers of Christ (Eph. 6:10-18). He constantly moves across the pages of the New Testament leaving a path of sin and destruction behind him. Parallel with the full revelation of Jesus as God's Son and our Saviour, is the full revelation of Satan as man's chief enemy and seducer.

III. HIS CHARACTER

The fundamental moral description of Satan is given by Jesus when he called him the "evil one" (Matt. 13:19, 38). Jehovah is described as the "holy one" (Isa. 6:3; Rev. 4:8), the embodiment of all that is good and holy. Satan is depicted as the one whose whole nature and will are given to evil. His vile character is seen in the following ways:

A. *He is a Liar*. Jesus said of Satan "He was a murderer from the beginning, and standeth not in the truth, because there is no truth in him. When he speaketh a lie he speaketh of his own for he is a liar and father thereof" (John 8:44). God is referred to as the God of Truth (Psa. 31:5), and Jesus as "the truth" (John 14:6). But Satan is called a liar and the father of lies.

It is clear from the Bible that a lie is the chief instrument Satan uses to work his wicked ways. Someone has said that Satan has many tools with which to do his work and a *lie* is the handle that fits each of them. His whole system is built upon

26

deceit and lying. The evil that lying does in the world is immeasurable. It was a lie that caused Adam and Eve to sin and bring suffering and death into the world. It was a lie that caused the prophet from Judah to be killed by a lion (I Kings 13:1-25). It was a lie that caused Ananias and Sapphira to lose their lives (Acts 5). The destiny of all liars like their father Satan will be "in the lake that burneth with fire and brimstone; which is the second death" (Rev. 21:8). This is the price one pays for obeying Satan.

B. *He is a murderer.* With a plain reference to Eden, Jesus calls Satan a murderer (John 8:44). Satan is a murderer because he originated the lie which brought sin into he world. The penalty for sin is death; therefore, he helped bring about the death of all men. One can only guess at the part Satan plays in the countless murders committed each year by individuals as well as those killed in wars. Satan's share in these atrocities must be great. John indicates Satan's involvement in sin when he writes, "he that doeth sin is of the devil; for the devil sinneth from the beginning" (I John 3:8).

C. *He is deceitful.* Satan is referred to as "the deceiver of the whole world" (Rev. 12:9, cf., 20:3; 8, 10, 13, 14). The word deceit is from a Greek word "delos" which originally meant "fish bait." As the fisherman decieves the fish by his lures or bait, so Satan deceives and catches the unwary by his wiles.

1. He deceives men about himself. During war the enemy uses great ingenuity to hide his real strength, hoping thereby to deceive his opponent and win the battle. It is not surprising that many people today including leading theologians do not believe in the existence of a powerful personality like Satan. This indicates how well he has concealed himself and deceived men into thinking he does not exist. The Bible, especially the New Testament, gives abundant proof that there is a powerful, personality directing the evil in the world. The evidence of his footprints across our land is so abundant that only the foolish and unwary could be deceived. The following poem illustrates this truth:

The Devil
Men don't believe in a devil now, as their fathers used
to do;

They've forced the door of the narrowest creed to let His
majesty through
There isn't a print of his cloven foot, or a fiery dart from
his bow
To be found in earth or air today, for the world has voted
it so.
We are told that he does not go about as a roaring lion
now:
But whom shall we hold responsible for the everlasting
row?
To be heard in home, in church, in state, to the earth's
remotest bound,
If the Devil by unanimous vote is nowhere to be found?
Who is it mixing the fatal drink that palsies heart and
brain?
And loads the bier of each passing year with a 100,000
slain.
Who dogs the steps of the toiling saint, and digs the pit
for his feet?
Who sows the tares in the field of time wherever God
sows His wheat?
Who blights the blooms of the land today with the fiery
breath of hell?
If the devil isn't and never was? Won't somebody rise
and tell!
The Devil is voted not to be, and, of course the thing is
true;
But who is doing the kind of work that the Devil used
to do?

    2. Satan deceives man concering his activities. He
tries to make his activities appear to be innocent and good. Paul
speaking of false teachers and deceitful workers said: "And no
wonder, for even Satan disguises himself as an angel of light. So
it is not strange if his servants also disguise themselves as servants of righteousness. Their end will correspond to their deeds"
(II Cor. 11:14-15 RSV; Cf. I John 4:1; II Thess. 2:9).

    Jesus in His parable of the Wheat and the Tares notes Sa-
tan's deceptive activity when he states that "while men slept, the

enemy came and sowed tares also among the wheat and went away" (Matt. 13:25). Satan tries to wrap his evil works in a cloak of goodness. Atheistic communism parades under the guize of helping the poor working man. The liquor industry boasts of the schools that are built by their tax money. No mention is made of the millions slaughtered and enslaved by the former or the sorrow and tragedies caused by the latter.

D. *He is Malicious.* His vicious nature can be seen in what he did to Adam and Eve. Our first parents were created holy and without sin. They enjoyed the beautiful garden and a close companionship with God. Satan by influencing them to sin, robbed them of their holiness, innocence, peace of mind, and eventually their lives. This is the malicious character with whom we have to deal.

His malicious nature is seen also in the physical affliction and financial loss he caused to Job and his family (Job 1:11-22; 2:4-7). In Luke 3:16, Jesus said that the crippled woman whom He healed had been bound by Satan. Paul's thorn in the flesh is said to have been "a messenger of Satan" to buffet or bruise him (II Cor. 12:7).

Satan snatches away the word of God sown in the hearts of the unsaved lest they believe it and escape his clutches (Matt. 13:19). He also blinds the minds of men to the gospel (II Cor. 4:3-4), and persuades them to accept his lie (II Thess. 2:9-10). Satan hinders the work of God's servants (I Thess. 2:18). Perhaps the most vivid description of Satan's malicious activity is recorded in I Peter 5:8 where Satan is described as a "roaring lion" walking or prowling about eagerly looking for someone to devour. Peter earnestly urges soberness, vigilance and steadfast resistance in order to keep this malicous being from destroying us.

IV. HIS WORK

A. *He is a ruler of a powerful and evil kingdom.* (Matt. 12:26; Luke 11:18). He is called the god of this world (II Cor. 4:4). The Greek word for world is *aion* which means "time world." Satan is the god of this time world. The implication is that his rule is temporary, and is limited to this present age (John 12:31).

29

Jesus speaks of Satan as the "prince of this world" (John 12:31; cf. John 14:30). The Greek word for world is *cosmos* which means "material world." This indicates that the principal area in which Satan works is the material realm.

Satan rules in two areas or realms. First, he is the leader of a vast organization of spirit-beings called "his angels" (Matt. 25:41). The Christian wrestles not against flesh and blood, "but against the principalities, against the powers, against the world-rulers of the darkness, against the spiritual hosts of wickedness in the heavenly places" (Eph. 6:12; cf., Col. 1:13). Satan leads a formidable and powerful host of evil spirits against the church. The Christian, however, does not fear, "because greater is He that is in you than he that is in the world" (I John 4:4).

Secondly, he exercises dominion over the world of lost humanity. John tells us that the whole world lieth in the evil one (I John 5:19). One does not need to look long at the tremendous sin in the world to be convinced that Satan is leading and controlling the lives of the majority of men.

B. *He is the Tempter of men.* Perhaps the best known work of Satan is his tempting men to do evil. No one escapes his temptations not even the Lord (Matt 4:3; cf., I Thess. 3:5; II Cor. 7:5). Jesus told Peter, "Simon, Simon, Behold Satan asked to have you, that he might sift you as wheat" (Luke 22:31).

The Bible says Satan tempts us. But James says "each man is tempted, when he is drawn away by his own lust, and enticed" (James 1:14). How can these two ideas be harmonized? A simple illustration may shed light o l how Satan tempts man, and yet man is responsible for his own actions in yielding to the temptations. When an angler places a lure on his hook and drops it in the water he hopes to deceive the fish into biting it. He is tempting the fish like Satan does man. However, the fish will not be caught unless by his own lust or desires he takes the bait. The Christian may see the lure of Satan but he will not sin or be caught unless he desires what Satan dangles before his eyes. Therefore, when he yields to the temptation he is to blame because the real impulse for the yielding came from within.

V.   SATAN CAN BE RESISTED

Satan is a powerful force in the world. John states that "the

30

whole world lieth in the evil one" (I John 5:19b). Yet he is not all powerful. He can be resisted because:

A. *God has limited his powers of temptation.* After warning the Christians at Corinth not to be overly confident in regards to sin Paul reassures them that "God is faithful; he will not suffer you to be tempted above that ye are able" (I Cor.10:13). God recognizes that Satan is more powerful than the Christian, and limits him so that he cannot by sheer force cause the Christian to yield to his temptations. God knows the amount of testing one can endure and in love forbids Satan to go beyond that limit. The trials of Job illustrate this point. God permitted Satan to try Job only as far as Job was able to endure (See Job :11-12; 2:6).

John reassures the Christian that Christ "who was born of God keeps him (the Christian), and the evil one does not touch him" (I John 5:18-RSV).

B. *Satan can be overcome if resisted.* God certainly does His part to keep Satan from overcoming the Christian but the Christian must also do his part in resisting temptations. James gives a plan for defeating Satan (James 4:7-8). He suggests these things:

1. Submit oneself to God's care.
2. Resist the devil—stand firm against him and he will flee.
3. Draw near to God with clean hands and pure hearts, and God will draw near with power and strength to overcome Satan.

VI. DESTINY OF SATAN

A. *Jesus came to destroy the works of Satan.* We read in Hebrews 2:14-15, "Since then the children are sharers in flesh and blood, he also himself in like manner partook of the same; that through death he might bring to nought him that had the power of death, that is, the devil; and might deliver all them who through fear of death were all their lifetime subject to bondage" (cf. I John 3:8).

When Christ arose from the dead he wrenched from Satan the weapon he held over the Christian, that is the fear of death. However, Satan was not destroyed but his power was limited. One might ask why God permits Satan to remain in the world.

31

Satan apparently is left to give man a choice between God and himself or good and evil. God permits Satan to test and tempt us for our own good. Trials and testings when overcome serve as a cleansing or purifying power. It strengthens character and prepares us for an eternal life with God (See Isa. 48:10; James 1:2-4, 12; Rev. 2:10).

     B. *The Lake of fire is his destiny.* Revelation 20:1-3 states that during the millenium, Satan will be bound for one thousand years and cast into the abyss. Following a short period of freedom, he will be cast into the lake of fire and brimstone along with the beast and false prophet to be tormented day and night forever (Rev. 20:7-10). This obviously is what Jesus had in mind when he said to the goats on his left hand, "depart from me ye cursed, into the eternal fire which is prepared for the devil and his angels" (Matt. 25:41). The devil will be destroyed and those who follow him will share his fate.

REVIEW QUESTIONS — SATAN

Fill in the Blanks:

1.   How many devils are there? _____.

2.   Satan means _____, or _____, and devil means

     _____, or _____.

3.   List three epithets for Satan: 1. _____

     2. _____, and 3. _____.

4.   What is the origin of Satan? _____

     _____

     _____

5.   What is Satan's chief instrument for evil? _____.

6.   List three ways that Satan's malicious nature is seen:

     1. _____, 2. _____

     _____, and 3. _____.

7.   Why does God allow Satan to remain on earth? _____

     _____

IV

HEAVEN

I. The Term Heaven in Scripture.
   A. The Atmospheric Heaven.
   B. The Stellar or Celestial Heaven.
   C. The Heaven of Heavens—The Dwelling Place of God.

II. Heaven—The Future Home of the Saints.
   A. A Country.
   B. A City.
   C. The Father's House.

III. Conditions in Heaven.
   A. Rest.
   B. Absence of Trouble and Sorrow.
   C. Abounding Life.
   D. Place of Service.

IV. Some Questions Concerning Heaven.
   A. What Kind of a Body will the Redeemed Have?
   B. Will We Know Each Other in Heaven?

V. Some People Who Will Not Be There.

VI. The Holy Fellowship of Those Who Will Be There.

HEAVEN

I. THE TERM HEAVEN IN SCRIPTURE

Heaven is usually thought of as referring to the future dwelling place of the righteous, however, the expression is used in a variety of ways in the Bible. The Apostle Paul speaks of the "third heaven" which he identified with Paradise (II Cor. 12:2-3). He evidently thought there were three heavens. The Bible identifies those three heavens in the following ways:

33

A. *The Atmospheric Heaven.* Genesis 1:6-8a says, "And God said, Let there be a firmament in the midst of the waters, and let it divide the waters from the waters. And God made the firmament, and divided the waters which were under the firmament from the waters which were above the firmament: and it was so. And God called the firmament Heaven." The word firmament refers to the atmosphere that surrounds this earth. This belt of air was to divide the water, which is on the earth from the water in the clouds above the earth (cf. Gen. 7:11; 8:2). In Genesis 1:20b God said, "Let birds fly above the earth in the open firmament of heaven." This blanket of air which we breathe is called the atmosphere and extends about twenty miles above the earth. This is the first heaven.

B. *The Stellar or Celestial Heaven.* A second way that the term heaven is used in the Bible is to identify the place of the sun, moon, and stars or what we call today "outer space." In scores of references to these heavenly bodies they are stated as being in the heavens. When God created the sun and moon He said, "Let there be lights in the firmament of heaven" (Gen. 1:14). The stars are said to be in heaven (Gen. 15:5; Deut. 4:19). David wrote in Psalms 8:3-4, "When I consider they heavens, the work of thy fingers, the moon and the stars, which thou hast ordained; What is man, that thou art mindful of him? And the son of man, that thou visiteth him?" The celestial bodies are in the second heaven.

C. *The Heaven of Heavens—the dwelling place of God.* God's abode is what most people think of as heaven. Even though the Scriptures teach that the "heaven of heavens" cannot contain God (I Kings 8:27; II Chron. 2:6), and that God is everywhere—"Do not I fill heaven and Earth? saith Jehovah" (Jer. 23:24; cf. Psa. 139:7-10), yet the Bible teaches clearly that He does dwell in a definite place called heaven (I Kings 8:39, 43, 49). Moses said in Deuteronomy 26:15, "Look down from thy holy habitation, from heaven, and bless thy people Israel." Psalms 103:19 states, "Jehovah hath established his throne in the heavens; and his kingdom ruleth over all" (cf. Psa. 11:4; Isa. 66:1; Matt. 5:34). Jesus taught his disciples to pray "Our Father who art in heaven, Hallowed be thy name" (Matt. 6:9). The Scriptures teach that God's saints will be with Him and Christ

34

in heaven throughout eternity (John 14:1-3, Rev. 21:1-4). This is the third heaven.

II. HEAVEN—THE FUTURE HOME OF THE SAINTS

Heaven is a real place where real people will go. This is scriptural teaching. Not everyone, though, believes this. Canon Farrar wrote, "heaven is to be something rather than to go somewhere." Patterson Smyth said, "Heaven means a state of character rather than a place of residence."[1] These men conceive of heaven as a state of character or mind achieved on earth rather than a place where one will live. They believe one creates his own heaven on earth by his thoughts and deeds.

The Bible speaks definitely of heaven as a place. For example, heaven is referred to as:

A. *A Country.* The Hebrew writer states that the Patriarchs considered themselves trangers and pilgrims on the earth and were seeking a homeland. He writes, "But now they desire a better country, that is, a heavenly: wherefore God is not ashamed of them, to be called their God" (Heb. 11:16).

In Philippians 3:20, Paul writes, "But we are citizens of Heaven; our outlook goes beyond this world to the hopeful expectation of the Saviour who will come from Heaven, the Lord Jesus Christ" (Phillips Translation). Referring to heaven as a country emphasizes one's citizenship in the kingdom of Heaven. Having entered the Redeemer's kingdom here on earth (Col. 1:13), the Christian if he is faithful to the end will be privileged to enter "the eternal kingdom of our Lord and Saviour Jesus Christ" (II Peter 1:11b).

The Christian is not truly at home in this world since Satan is now the god of this world (II Cor. 4:1; cf. John 12:31; John 14:30). Someday by God's Grace the redeemed will go to their "own" country where God is King. Joyfully we sing in anticipation:

This world is not my home, I'm just passing through.
My treasures are laid up somewhere beyond the blue.
The angels beckon me from Heaven's opened door,
And I can't feel at home in this world any more.

---

[1]*20th Century Christian,* Edited by Norvel Young, April, 1958, p. 4.

35

B. *A City*. A second description of heaven is as a city. The idea of a city of God, blessed by His presence and existing forever, goes back to the Patriarchal Period when God began to prepare a people for Himself. Abraham is said to have "looked for the city which hath the foundations, whose builder and maker is God" (Heb. 11:10). Hebrews 11:16b states that God, "hath prepared for them a city." The Psalmist echoed this hope when he wrote: "There is a river, the streams whereof make glad the city of God, the holy place of the tabernacles of the Most High. God is in the midst of her; she shall not be moved: God will help her, and that right early" (Psa. 46:4-5).

John called this city, "the holy city" (Rev. 21:2). This is in contrast to the unholy cities on earth. This is essential if God, the Holy One, is to dwell there. For God will not dwell where sin is. God's purpose in the whole plan of redemption is to make man holy. Heaven is the logical climax of this purpose.

John adds the modifier, "new Jerusalem" (Rev. 21:2). This implies that old Jerusalem in Palestine is a type of the church in her glorified state. Paul speaks of heaven as "the Jerusalem that is above is free, which is our mother" (Gal. 4:26). Hebrews 12:22, referring to the destiny of God's saints, says "Ye are come unto Mt. Zion, and unto the city of the living God, the heavenly Jerusalem . . ." (cf. Rev. 3:12). Heaven is thus termed a spiritual mountain and a city (cf. Gal. 4:21-31).

Description of the New Jerusalem. The apostle John gives a full description of the New Jerusalem which he saw descending from heaven (Rev. 21:9-27; 22:1-5). Here is the city as he saw it:

1. *Dimensions*. The City is a perfect cube like the Holy of Holies in the tabernacle and in Solomon's Temple (I Kings 6:19-20). It is 12,000 furlongs long, wide, and high (Rev. 21:16). This would be, in our measurements, 1,500 miles square and 1,500 miles high. If this city were placed in the United States it would reach from Atlanta, Georgia on the east to Denver, Colorado on the west; and from Montreal, Canada on the north to Key West, Florida on the south.

There are two lessons to be learned from these dimensions. First, heaven is perfect. A cube is considered the perfect geometrical form. An examination of it in Revelation 21 and 22 convinces one that it is a perfect place.

Second, it is a large place. The size of the city is tremendous. The city of Atlanta, Georgia covers 135 square miles. The New Jerusalem covers 2,250,000 square miles—over 16,000 times as large as Atlanta. It is 20 times as large as all New Zealand, and 10 times as large as Germany.

Obviously, our Heavenly Father is expecting a lot of His children to come home. Hebrews 12:22 speaks of an innumerable host of angels plus the Church of the firstborn assembled in the heavenly Jerusalem. When one considers that the redeemed of all ages will be there plus those who die in infancy it is easy to see that there will be a great host in heaven.

2. *Wall.* Surrounding this city is a great wall made of jasper. The thickness of the wall is 144 cubits (Rev. 17-18). If the cubit were 18 inches then the city wall would be 216 feet thick! Modern cities do not have walls. But the ancients would have considered the description of a city incomplete without a wall.

3. *The Foundations of the Wall.* There will be 12 foundations underneath the great wall of the New Jerusalem. These are formed from all manner of precious stones. "The first foundation was jasper; the second, sapphire, the third, chalcedony; the fourth, emerald; the fifth, sardonyx; the sixth, sardius, the seventh, chrysolite; the eighth, beryl; the ninth, topaz; the tenth, chrysoprase, the eleventh, jacinth; the twelfth, amethyst" (Rev. 21:19-20).

An artist one time was interested in the color scheme presented by these twelve foundations. He obtained a sample of each of these precious stones. He wanted to see if the colors would clash, stand out or be harmonious. When he laid the stones out in the exact order described in Revelation, he found that there was a perfect blending of colors. One more testimony to the perfection of God's work.

4. *Gates.* The great wall of the new Jerusalem is pierced by 12 gates; 3 on the east; 3 on the west; 3 on the south; and 3 on the north (Rev. 21:13). The 12 gates are 12 pearls. "Each one of the several gates was of one pearl" (Rev. 21:21). On each gate is written the name of one of the 12 tribes of Israel

(Rev. 21:12). An angel stands at each gate which leads into the New Jerusalem.

The gates remain open continually. They are not shut by day nor by night since there is no night there. They are not closed against thieves and murderers because there are none there. The 12 gates symbolize abundant and free entrance to the heavenly city.

5. *The streets.* "And the street of the city was pure gold, as it were transparent glass" (Rev. 21:21). The street harmonizes with the rest of the city for John writes in Revelation 21:18, "and the city was pure gold, like unto pure glass."

Whether or not the heavenly city will be made of gold, jasper, and pearl as we know them is uncertain. It is certain that God has used the most precious terms that man can understand in order to convey to him the glories of heaven. If it is not real gold as we know it, it will certainly be even more precious than that. The point is that heaven will be more wonderful than anything that man can imagine.

6. *Lights.* "And the city hath no need of the sun, neither of the moon, to shine upon it: for the glory of God did lighten it, and the lamp thereof is the Lamb" (Rev. 21:23). An illustration of the great light that surrounds God and Christ can be seen in the appearance of Jesus to Paul on the road to Demascus. When Christ appeared the brightness of His glory was said to have been, "above the brightness of the sun . . ." (Acts 26:13). It was so bright that Paul and his company fell to the ground. It seems to have been the cause of Paul's blindness (Acts 22:11; cf. Acts 9:8-9).

A similar illustration of the glory of God can be seen on the Mount of Transfiguration. Mark records that when Christ was transfigured, "His clothes became dazzling white, with a whiteness no bleacher on earth could equal" (Mark 9:3 NEB). As compared to this glory light the sun would look like a candle compared to an electric light. Heaven will be filled with light (Rev. 21:23; cf. Rev. 22:5).

7. *No Temple.* John tells us in Revelation 21:22, "and I saw no temple therein: for the Lord God the Almighty, and the Lamb, are the temple thereof." Such things as altars, temples, the Lord's Supper, etc. are substitutes for the reality

which is God and Christ. They are reminders or means through which we worship God. In heaven we will need none of these reminders or substitutes. We will be able to see and know God and Christ and worship and praise them throughout eternity (I John 3:2). Truly a marvelous city—the eternal home of God's saints!

C. *The Father's House.* The third description of heaven is a very personal term—"the Father's House." In comforting his disciples Jesus told them that in his Father's House were many mansions awaiting them. The word mansions literally means "abiding places." On earth man is pictured as a wanderer seeking a better city, a better country. In the Father's House the Christian will be at home. There will be no more wandering; his quest will be over. God shall dwell with them, "and they shall see his face" (Rev. 21:3; 22:4). Home is where Father is. Heaven will be as real as God is because it is His home.

This is the warmest and most personal description of heaven. Men may find it difficult to relate to the word "country" or "city" since these can be rather cold, impersonal terms. But every man can relate intellectually and emotionally to home. The Father's House reminds us of an earthly home where mother and father and brothers and sisters and warmth and love were. Death, to the Christian, will be going home to where his loved ones are.

III. CONDITIONS IN HEAVEN

God not only makes heaven appealing to man through the description of the place, but He also pictures it as a place where wonderful conditions exist. Here are a few of them:

A. *Rest.* "And I heard a voice from heaven saying, Write, Blessed are the dead who die in the Lord from henceforth: yea, saith the Spirit, that they may rest from their labors; for their works follow with them" (Rev. 14:13). This blessed rest is for those who die "in the Lord." This is in contrast to the wicked who are described as being in restless torment (Luke 16:23-24; cf. Rev. 20:10). Most of our labor and wrestling in this world is against sin (Eph. 6:10-13). In heaven there will be no Satan to oppose us or sin to tempt us. This will certainly be a blessed rest.

B. *Absence of Trouble and Sorrow.* In Revelation 21:4, God is pictured as a loving parent comforting and soothing His children. John writes: "he shall wipe away every tear from their eyes; and death shall be no more; neither shall there be mourning, nor crying, nor pain, any more: the first things are passed away." Sin is the cause of most of the tears, mournings, and death on earth. With sin and Satan absent these will not be in heaven.

Revelation 22:3 states, "And there shall be no curse any more." This apparently refers to the curse God laid upon Adam, Eve, the serpent, and the ground after the sin in the Garden of Eden (Gen. 3:16-19). The curse has been eliminated because Christ paid the penalty for sin. There will be no curse in the new Garden of Eden—"the Paradise of God" (Rev. 2:7).

C. *Abounding Life.* The abundant life in heaven is symbolized by the river of life and the tree of life. Rivers in the middle east have always been sources of life, physically speaking, for the nations. A look at a map will show that life bloomed along the Nile, the Tigris, and Euphrates Rivers.

This is more or less true all over the world. John's vision included, "a river of water of life, bright as crystal, proceeding out of the throne of God and of the Lamb, in the midst of the street thereof" (Rev. 22:1-2a). Life on this earth began beside a river (Gen. 2:10). Man's eternal life will continue by the River of Life. It is interesting that Jesus speaks of the spiritual life which He gives to man as being water (John 4:10-14). The Holy Spirit is spoken of as a river of living water flowing out of man (John 7:37-39).

The other symbol of abounding life in heaven is the tree of life. The tree of life is filled with abundant fruit, producing a crop each month. "On either side of the river stood a tree of life, which yields twelve crops of fruit, one for each month of the year. The leaves of the trees serve for the healing of the nations, and every accursed thing shall disappear" (Rev. 22:2-NEB). This fruit will provide abundant life for every soul in heaven. The leaves are said to be beneficial for sustaining health. This indicates that man will be provided with everything he will need throughout eternity.

D. *Place of Service.* "And His servants shall serve Him"

40

(Rev. 22:3b). John described those who had come out of the great tribulation and washed their robes white in the blood of the Lamb as attending constantly before the throne of God and "they serve him day and night in His temple" (Rev. 7:15). The word service of course includes worship and praise. It seems, though, that there will be work for the redeemed to do. Just what this service will be is not stated. But it will certainly be something that man will enjoy doing just the same as he enjoys working for God here on earth.

Much more could be said about heaven—its beauty, its holiness, its fellowship, its joys. Someone has said that "it would be punishment enough for the wicked just to miss heaven." One cannot afford to do that!

"Think of . . .
Stepping on shore, and finding it heaven!
Of taking hold of a hand, and finding it God's hand;
Of breathing a new air, and finding it celestial air;
Of feeling invigorated, and finding it immortality;
Of passing from storm and tempest to an unbroken calm;
Of waking up, and finding it home."[1]

IV.   SOME QUESTIONS CONCERNING HEAVEN

Many questions are asked regarding life in heaven. Most of these questions cannot be answered since God has not seen fit to give the answer in His Word. But here are a few of the questions and at least partial answers to them.

A.   *What Kind of a Body Will the Redeemed Have?* In speaking of our new bodies Paul said that when Christ comes again, "He will re-make these wretched bodies of ours so that they resemble His own glorious body, by that power of His which makes Him the Master of everything that is" (Phil. 3:21-Phillips). John tells us, "when He shall appear, we shall be like Him; for we shall see him as he is" (I John 3:2-KJV). Revelation 22:4 states, "and they shall see His face; and His name shall be on their foreheads."

---

[1]*20th Century Christian*, April, 1958, p. 5.

41

These scriptures indicate that our bodies will be similar to Christ's glorified body and that we shall be able to see Him and the heavenly Father since we will be like them. Paul calls the new body a "spiritual body" (I Cor. 15:44). It will be a real body but one that is suited to our spiritual existence in heaven. In I Corinthians 15:42-44, Paul describes the new body. He says it will be imperishable or incorruptible, glorious, powerful, and spiritual. These four words are the best description of the new body found in the New Testament. For its exact looks and nature we must wait until by God's grace we receive it.

B. *Will We Know Each Other in Heaven?* The scriptures indicate that only the body, not the spirit, is changed in the death of the Christian. The physical body is exchanged for the new "spiritual body." As far as the spirit of man (the real person) is concerned, it remains the same. On the Mount of Transfiguration (Matt. 17:1-8), Moses and Elijah appeared and talked with Jesus concerning His death in Jerusalem (Luke 9:31). They appeared in "glory" but were still Moses and Elijah.

In the parable of the Rich Man and Lazarus (Luke 16:19-31), Lazarus and Abraham were recognized by the rich man in Hades. When God appeared to Moses on Mount Horeb to send him to Egypt He said, "I am the God of thy Father, the God of Abraham, the God of Isaac, and the God of Jacob" (Ex. 3:6). All of these men had been dead for centuries, yet God speaks of them as still living and as being the same persons (See Matthew 22:31-32).

Some have questioned how we would recognize each other since we will have new glorified bodies. In this physical world we rely on the physical appearance in recognizing each other. Presumably, in our spiritual existence in heaven we will be recognized by our "person" or spirit which is the real person anyway. In this life man is a spirit dwelling in a physical body. There he will be a spirit dwelling in a spiritual body. There should be no more difficulty recognizing each other there than there is here on earth.

V. SOME PEOPLE WHO WILL NOT BE THERE

Some believe that everyone will go to heaven regardless of

his spiritual condition. In the *London Daily Mail*, October 2, 1961, Archbishop of Canterbury, Arthur Michael Ramsey, head of the Church of England and President of he World Council of Churches said, "Heaven is not a place to which humans go in our present bodily state nor is it a place for Christians only! Those who have led a good life on earth but found themselves unable to believe in God will not be debarred from heaven. I expect to meet some present day atheists there." Paul, however, takes no such view of the atheist and his rejection of God. He says that the evidence for God is so clear that men who refuse to believe it have no possible defense for their conduct (Rom. 1:20-NEB).

Other scriptures agree that some people will not make it to heaven. After listing the works of the flesh such as fornication, idolatry, envyings, drunkenness, and such like, Paul states, "of which I forewarn you, even as I did forewarn you, that they who practice such things shall not inherit the Kingdom of God" (Gal. 5:19-21). "And there shall in no wise enter into it anything unclean, or he that maketh an abomination and a lie: but only they that are written in the Lamb's book of life" (Rev. 21:27). "But for the fearful, and unbelieving, and abominable, and murderers, and fornicators, and sorcerers, and idolaters, and all liars, their part shall be in the lake that burneth with fire and brimstone: which is the second death" (Rev. 21:8). "And to you that are afflicted rest with us, at the revelation of the Lord Jesus from heaven with the angels of his power in flaming fire, rendering vengeance to them that know not God, and to them that obey not the gospel of our Lord Jesus: who shall suffer punishment, even eternal destruction from the face of the Lord and from the glory of his might" (II Thess. 1:7-9).

These scriptures clearly teach that heaven is a prepared place for those who are prepared to go there. This preparation includes accepting Jesus as God's son and our Messiah and Saviour. This acceptance, of course, involves a complete trust or faith in Him, and a forsaking of sin through repentance. It also includes confessing Christ before men, and being immersed into Him (Mark 16:15-16; Rom. 10:-10; Acts 2:38). In order to enter heaven we must also be faithful unto death if we are to receive the crown of life (Rev. 2:10; cf. Rev. 2:7).

43

VI. THE HOLY FELLOWSHIP OF THOSE WHO WILL BE THERE

Words cannot describe the joy it will be to live in heaven. Hebrews 12:22-23 mentions the "innumerable hosts of angels", and the "church of the firstborn who are enrolled in heaven, and to God the Judge of all, and to the spirits of just men made perfect." Jesus our Saviour will be there to welcome us home.

Jesus said, "many shall come from the east and the west, and shall sit down with Abraham, and Isaac, and Jacob, in the Kingdom of Heaven" (Matt. 8:11). Revelation 5:11 describes the great number surrounding God's throne as "ten thousand times ten thousand, and thousands of thousands."

What a privilege it will be to join with the redeemed of all ages in singing praises to God and to the Lamb. All the pure, the holy, and the blessed servants of God will be there. Just to enjoy the presence of God and of Christ and to live in the light of their glory will be indescribable. This is why Paul said, "for I reckon that the sufferings of this present time are not worthy to be compared with the glory which shall be revealed to us-ward" (Rom. 8:18).

REVIEW QUESTIONS—HEAVEN

Fill in the Blanks:

1. What are the three Heavens mentioned in the Bible?

    a. _____

    b. _____

    c. _____

2. What lessons can be learned from the size and shape of the new Jerusalem?

    a. _____

    _____

    b. _____

    _____

3. The following are made of what materials?

   a. Walls _____

   b. Streets _____

   c. Gates _____

4. What type of bodies will the redeemed have in heaven? _____

   _____

5. The abundant life in heaven is symbolized by:

   a. _____

   b. _____

V

HELL

I. What is Hell?
   A. Four words translated Hell.
   B. History of the Valley of Hinnom.

II. The Nature of Hell.
   A. Jesus' description of Hell.
   B. Other descriptions in the New Testament.
   C. The significance of these descriptions.

III. The Existence of Hell.
   A. Reason demands it.
   B. Justice requires it.
   C. Revelation reveals it.

IV. The Duration of Hell.
   A. Abbreviated punishment.
   B. Annihilation.
   C. Eternal.

V. The inhabitants of Hell.

VI. Hell is not for the Christian.

HELL

Man is naturally reluctant to think about judgment and punishment. He likes to think of God's blessings and rewards but not his punishments.

Because of this many schemes have been invented to escape the reality that man will suffer for unforgiven sins. Some think that hell is only the hurt man experiences from a guilty conscience when he does wrong. Others claim that all the hell we get will be here on earth. Man makes his own hell by the way he lives. These same people seem to be in favor of a place called heaven. But the same Scriptures that speak of heaven speak also of hell. If we do not receive our heaven here on earth then we do not receive our hell here either.

Let it be said in the beginning that no man goes to hell because God wants him to go. For God is "not willing that any should perish, but that all should come to repentance" (II Pet. 3:9). Neither does any man go to hell because there is no escape. For God in his love and mercy has prepared the way of escape. That way is through Jesus Christ (Heb. 2:14-15; cf. John 14:6). "Every sinner who goes to hell walks over the body of Jesus Christ, tramples 'the blood of the covenant' under his feet and passes unconcerned by the cross which, as a flaming beacon, stands squarely in the way of every perdition-bent individual. If you go to hell, my sinner friend, don't blame God or His Son."[1] God's whole effort has been to save man from hell so that the individual who is lost has no one to blame but himself.

I. WHAT IS HELL

The first question to answer is: "what is hell?" There are four words in the Bible (King James Version) which are translated hell. Their meanings will help clarify the Bible teaching on hell.

A. *Four words translated Hell:*

1. *Sheol*—In the Old Testament the Hebrew word *Sheol* is translated "hell" a number of times (Psa. 9:17; 16:10; Jonah 2:2). In Genesis 37:35 the same word is translated "grave." Numbers 16:30 translates *Sheol* as "pit."

Sometimes this word has the connotation of punishment but mostly the word refers to the "grave" or the "abode of the dead" without necessarily referring to punishment. For example Psalms 16:10, which is a prophecy of Jesus, says, "For thou wilt not leave my soul in hell (Sheol); Neither wilt thou suffer Thine Holy One to see corruption" (KJV). Peter quotes this in Acts 2:31 as referring to Jesus' temporary abode between His death and His resurrection. Many modern versions use the word *Sheol* instead of hell in most references in the Old Testament. This is

---

[1]Kellems, Jessee, *The Resurrection Gospel*, p. 60.

47

because the word does not refer to the future place of punishment.

2. *Hades*—The word *Hades* in the New Testament is synonymous with the word *Sheol* in the Old Testament. In Acts 2:31 Peter uses the Greek word *Hades* to translate the Hebrew word *Sheol*. The word *Hades* literally means "unseen, covered, or unseen world." It refers to the abode of the dead, not to the eternal place of punishment (cf. Matt. 11:23; 16:18; Luke 16:23; I Cor. 15:55).

3. *Tartarus*—This word appears one time in the New Testament in II Peter 2:4. "For if God spared not angels when they sinned, but cast them down to hell (Tartarus), and committed them to pits of darkness, to be reserved unto judgment . . ." Whether this prison for the fallen angels is the same as hell is not clear. Some think it is the section of Hades where the wicked go. It may be a special place prepared for the wicked angels (cf. Jude 6).

4. *Gehenna*—The word *Gehenna* is a combination of two Aramaic words *ge* meaning "valley" and *Hinnom* which was evidently the name of some man. It means the "valley of Hinnom." This word Gehenna is consistently translated "hell" in the New Testament. It is used twelve times. Eleven times it is used by Jesus Himself. One time it is used by James the Lord's brother (James 3:6). Here are the references: Matt. 5:22; 29, 30; 10:28; 18:9; 23:15; 23:33; Mark 9:43; 45, 47; Luke 12:5. In all these instances the word refers to the place of future punishment.

Why did Jesus use the name of a valley in Palestine as the name for the place of punishment for the wicked? A study of the valley will answer this question.

B. *History of the Valley of Hinnom.* Solomon introduced idolatry to Jerusalem when he erected a high place or altar of worship on Mount Olivet to the god Molech. He did this to please his foreign wives (I Kings 11:7). Later under the evil kings Ahaz, Manasseh, and Amon the valley of Hinnom was made the scene of gross and cruel rites of heathen worship (II Chron. 28:1-3; 33:1-9, 21-25). The valley of Hinnom was located southwest of the city of Jerusalem. With the leadership of these kings the Jews built the image of Molech and sacrificed to it in the valley of Hinnom. The image of Molech was a large, hollow, brazen figure with the body of a man and the head of a calf. It had large arms and hands extended from the body. A fire was built inside the image and heated until red hot. The worshippers would then place an infant in the hands of the idol as a sacrifice. It is said that they beat drums to drown out the cries of the infant. Other authorities believe the baby was killed and then burned as a sacrifice. This is what is meant when the Scriptures talk about passing their children through the fire to Molech (II Kings 16:2-4; 21:1-6).

This cruel and monstrous worship was an abomination to God. When King Josiah came to the throne of Judah, he killed the idolatrous priests and stopped this worship. He tore down the altars, cut down the groves, and thoroughly abolished the valley and its evil worship (II Kings 23:1-20). "And they brake down the altars of the Baalim in his presence; and the sun-images that were on high above them he hewed down; and the Asherim, and the graven images, and the molten imagies, he brake in pieces, and made dust of them, and strewed it upon the graves of them that had sacrificed unto them. And he burnt the bones of the priests upon their altars, and purged Judah and Jerusalem" (II Chron. 34:4-5).

After it's pollution by Josiah, "it became an object of horror to the Jews, and is said to have been made a receptable for bones, the bodies of beasts and criminals, refuse and all unclean things. The terrible associations of the place, the recollections of the horrors perpetrated in it, and the defilement inflicted on it, the fires said to have been kept burning in it in order to consume the foul and corrupt objects that were thrown into it, made it a natural and unmistakable symbol of dire evil, torment, wasting penalty, absolute ruin."[1]

The valley of Hinnom consequently became associated in prophecy with the judgment to be visited upon the people of Judah (Jer. 7:31-32). When Jesus desired to tell his disciples what hell would be like he pointed to the Valley of Hinnom and said,

---

[1]*A Dictionary of the Bible*, Edited by James Hastings, Volume 2, p. 344.

"Hell will be like that." It was a most graphic illustration. This is why the word *Gehenna* is translated "hell" and does refer to the future punishment of the wicked.

II. THE NATURE OF HELL

A. *Jesus's description of hell.* Eleven times in the Synoptic Gospels Jesus refers to the nature of hell. He speaks of hell as "eternal fire", and as "hell of fire", or "Gehenna of fire" (Matt. 18:8-9). He calls it the "unquenchable fire" (Mark 9:43). In Mark 9:48 Jesus says, "the fire is not quenched." He called hell, "eternal punishment" (Matt. 25:46); "where their worm dieth not" (Mark 9:48). It will be a place of "weeping and gnashing of teeth" (Matt. 8:12). It is a place of great sorrow and great anger.

The wicked who go to hell will be banished from the presence of Christ (Matt. 7:23; cf. II Thess. 1:9). Finally, Jesus describes hell as a place of utter or outer darkness (Matt. 25:30). Elsewhere the final destiny of the unrighteous is described in the following terms.

B. *Other descriptions of Hell in the New Testament.* It is pictured as "the mist of darkness" (KJV); "blackest darkness" (TCNT); or "densest darkness" (Weymouth) (II Pet. 2:17). Jude 13, speaks of the wicked, "for whom the blackness of darkness hath been reserved forever" (cf. Jude 6).

The Hebrew writer warns us in Hebrews 10:26-27, "For if we sin willfully after that we have received the knowledge of the truth, there remaineth no more a sacrifice for sins, but a certain fearful expectation of judgment, and a fierceness of fire which shall devour the adversaries." In that same chapter and in verse 39 he refers to the destiny of the wicked as "perdition" or "destruction." Hell is also called "the lake that burneth with fire and brimstone" (Rev. 21-8; 20:10; 19:20). In this connection hell is referred to as the second death—the eternal death for those who reject the Gospel (Rev. 20:6, 14; 21:8). The promise to the righteous is: "He that overcometh shall not be hurt of the second death" (Rev. 2:11).

Other descriptions of hell in the New Testament are "wrath and indignation, tribulation, and anguish" (Rom. 2:8-9);

"death" (Rom. 6:21); "perdition" (destruction) (Phil. 3:19); "eternal destruction from the face of the Lord" (II Thess. 1:9).

C. *The significance of these descriptions.* When the Bible speaks of heaven it uses the most beautiful terms in the human language: streets of gold, gates of pearl, walls of jasper. God has used every means to persuade men to strive for heaven. On the other hand, when the Bible speaks of hell it uses the most fearful and awful words that are known to man. God has chosen two things in describing hell that are feared by most men—fire and complete darkness.

1. *Fire.* When we come near fire we immediately recoil from it knowing the pain that it can inflict upon the human body. We shudder when we even think of being burned in fire. Whether the fire of hell will be actual fire as we know it here on earth, we do not know. If it is not literal fire, it evidently will be a suffering as bad or worse than fire. God has used this description of hell to discourage men from even thinking of going to hell.

2. *Darkness.* The second description that God uses is the term darkness—"outer darkness"—"blackness of darkness." There is a certain dread and fear about complete darkness. Some years ago I had the opportunity to visit the Mammoth Caves in Kentucky. The guide led us on a tour down into the depths of the earth. There we came to a large room and stopped to rest; far below we could hear the river thundering through the heart of the earth. The guide asked us if we had ever seen darkness. We said yes. He said he would show us some *real* darkness. He then switched off the electric lights. For a short time everyone was exclaiming about the darkness. They had fun bringing their hands up to their faces in an effort to see their hands. It was impossible to see anything! This continued for perhaps half a minute. And then suddenly there seemed to be a certain dread begin to creep into the hearts of each one. Through my mind flew the thought, what if the electric lights do not come back on? I thought of that dark river below and the chasms we had crossed coming down. There seemed to be a heavy weight begin to press down upon us. I have never been so happy to see light as I was when the guide pressed the switch and the room

flooded with light. Hell is said to have this complete, oppressive darkness!

Some would question how there could be fire and darkness in hell at the same time. I do not try to harmonize these two because we actually know so little about the exact nature of hell, what kind of fire, darkness, etc. I would suggest that God is using every description he can to help man understand what an awful place hell is, so that he will accept Jesus as his Saviour and not go there.

III. THE EXISTENCE OF HELL

The evidence for a place called hell is abundant in the Scriptures. Our Lord and the Apostles both testify to that fact. There is much that we do not know about hell but that there is a place where the wicked will go is very clearly presented. Yet many people today reject the idea of a place of future punishment for the wicked. Several years ago a professor at Northwest University in Chicago, Dr. George Herbert Betts, wrote a book entitled, *The Beliefs of 700 Ministers.*[1] This book was the result of a questionnaire he sent out to fifteen hundred ministers of the Midwest area. Seven hundred replies were received. Among this number there were two hundred students from five theological schools. One of the questions which Dr. Betts asked the two hundred students was: "Do you believe that hell exists as an actual place or location?" Here is the response of these potential religious leaders: 76% answered No; 13% were uncertain; and only 11% believed in hell. The sobering fact is that the same Lord who said there is a heaven also said there is a hell. Here are three reasons for believing in hell as the eternal destiny of the wicked.

A. *Reason demands it.* If the Scriptures had nothing to say about hell, common sense and reason would lead a person to conclude the necessity for such a place anyway. Logically, there cannot really be a heaven without a hell. If heaven is to be a holy place where peace and righteousness prevail, then there must be a place for the wicked to go. If all the criminals of the earth were placed in heaven it would soon be changed to a hell itself. If a modern city is to be clean and healthful it must have

---

[1]Betts, G.H., *The Beliefs of 700 Ministers,* (Abingdon Press), p. 55.

52

a garbage dump, a waste disposal, and a sewage system. By the same token if heaven is to be clean and holy then the unclean of this earth must be placed somewhere else. That place is called Hell in the Bible.

B. *Justice requires it.* Several years ago the English Jurist, Sir William Blackstone wrote, "Where there is no penalty the law is null and void."

"If there is no hell or penalty, then there is no law, for 'law without penalty is null and void.' If there is no law, then there is no sin, for 'where there is no law, there can be no wrong, or violation'."[1]

Fact number one—there is a law of God written in the Bible. Fact number two—men break those laws and sin, thus causing much suffering and evil in the world. The reasonable conclusion is that there must be punishment for sin. God is both righteous and reasonable and His word declares that there is a punishment for unforgiven sin—hell.

There is another reason why justice requires a judgment and a place of punishment. That is because of the sin and crimes that go unpunished in this life. By way of illustration, there was an article in a Chicago newspaper dated July 24, 1943, that carried this headline, "Half of 5,133 murders in the city since 1925 unsolved."[2] This article goes on to say that for a period of eighteen years prior to this there had been 5,133 murders committed in the city of Chicago. Yet, after eighteen years, less than 50% of them had been solved, which meant that most of them never would be solved or punished here on earth! Will these murders never be judged? Will the criminals who committed them never be punished? Will a righteous God go on allowing men to shake their fists in His face, break His laws, and never pay for their sins? Not if God is righteous and omnipotent! And He is. Therefore, we conclude that justice requires the existence of hell to punish the wicked who escape punishment in this life.

C. *Revelation Reveals It.* We have already given many scriptures speaking of the reality of hell, the terrible conditions

---

[1]Kellems, J.R., *The Resurrection Gospel,* (Standard Publishing Company, 1924), p. 66.

[2]Smith, Wilbur, *Therefore Stand,* (W.A. Wilde Company, 1945), p. 456.

of hell, and the people who will go there. Eleven times our Lord speaks of Gehenna. To the individual who believes that the Bible is the Word of God then there can be no reasonable doubt that there is a place where the wicked will go at the end of this life. The Bible calls that place Hell.

IV. THE DURATION OF HELL

A. *Abbreviated punishment*. Down through the ages men have tried to eliminate hell completely or else have tried to shorten it. For example, Hillel the famous Jewish teacher taught that sinful Gentiles would be punished in Gehenna for a space of twelve months and then be consumed. He did not believe that Jews went to hell.

The doctrine of purgatory teaches that a person who leaves this life unfit for heaven may go into an intermediate state called purgatory where he may be cleansed or purged of his wickedness. The he will be admitted to Heaven.

The Scriptures, of course, know nothing about these abbreviated punishments. Jesus said to the goats on His left (the wicked ones), "Depart from me ye cursed, into the eternal fire" (Matt. 25:41). Again He said: "And these (goats) shall go away into eternal punishment: but the righteous into eternal life" (Matt. 25:46). Jesus used the same Greek word in both instances. It is *aionios* and means "everlasting" or "eternal." The duration of the punishment for the wicked is the same as the duration of bliss for the righteous.

B. *The Doctrine of Annihilation*. Those who hold this view believe that the wicked will be extinguished like a light. They will cease to exist as conscious, living beings and will be completely destroyed. This is based on Paul's statement in II Thessalonians 1:9. Paul writes that the wicked will "suffer punishment even eternal destruction from the face (presence) of the Lord and from the glory of His might." They say the word destruction means annihilation. The Greek word translated "destruction" does not necessarily mean "annihilation." Moulton and Milligan in *Vocabulary of the Greek Testament*, define its first century Biblical usage as follows: "ruin, the loss of all that gives worth to existence."

Arndt and Gingrich in their *A Greek-English Lexicon*, give the meaning as "destruction, ruin, death."

Instead of annihilation the word means the ruin or destruction of all that gives worth or meaning to existence. "The eternal condition of the lost will be one of utter ruin, a condition in which the soul lives forever in a state devoid of all that makes existence worthwhile."[1]

C. *Eternal Punishment*. Other scriptures on hell seem definitely to teach a conscious existence after death for the wicked. For example, Jesus states in Mark 9:48 that the "fire is not quenched and the worm dieth not." This certainly seems to teach a continuous existence in hell.

The second death for the wicked will be their final separation from the presence of God (Rev. 20:14-15). Paul states: "They will suffer the punishment of eternal ruin, cut off from the presence of the Lord and the splendour of his might" (II Thess. 1:9-NEB).

V. THE INHABITANTS OF HELL

Jesus said that hell is prepared for the devil and his angels (Matt. 25:41). Hell was not prepared for man. If man goes to hell he will go because he has followed Satan to "his" home instead of following Jesus to the "Father's house."

The Scriptures indicate a very wicked and unholy population in hell. II Thessalonians 1:8-9 states that two groups will be there. First, those who know not God, obviously because they have rejected Him (cf. Rom. 1:28), and second, those who obey not the Gospel of the Lord Jesus Christ. Revelation 21:8 gives a more specific list of those who will be there: "But for the fearful, and unbelieving, and abominable, and murderers, and fornicators, and sorcerers, and idolaters, and all liars, their part shall be in the lake that burneth with fire and brimstone; which is the second death." The Apostle Paul adds: "Now the works of the flesh are plain: immorality, impurity, licentiousness, idolatry, sorcery, enmity, strife, jealousy, anger, selfishness, dissension, party spirit, envy, drunkenness, carousing, and the like. I warn

---

[1]Wuest, Kenneth S., *Treasures From the Greek New Testament* (W.B. Eerdmans Publishing Company, 1941), p. 41.

you, as I warned you before that those who do such things shall not inherit the kingdom of God" (Gal. 5:19-21-RSV). Obviously, if they do not inherit the Kingdom of God, this black list of sinners will end up in hell.

In summary, Satan and his angels will be there as will all the wicked who refuse to accept Christ. The dregs of the earth, spiritually speaking, of all ages will be collected in this cesspool of iniquity. R.G. Lee in his poem, "Hell, the Prisonhouse of Despair" describes some of the conditions:

"Hell the prisonhouse of despair
Here are some things that will be there.
Fire and brimstone are there we know
For God in His word hath told us so.
Memory, remorse, suffering and pain
Weeping and wailing, but all in vain.
Blasphemers, swearers, haters of God
Christ rejectors, while here they trod.
Murderers, gamblers, drunkards and liars—
Will have their part in the Lake of Fire.
The filthy, the vile, the cruel, and the mean
What a horrible mob in hell will be seen!"

VI.   HELL IS NOT FOR THE CHRISTIAN

However horrible hell may be, the grand news is that this is not the destiny of the Christian. "For our citizenship is in heaven; whence also we wait for a Saviour, the Lord Jesus Christ" (Phil. 3:20).

This is true because Jesus Christ our Saviour came and died on the Cross for our sins. He then arose from the grave and "abolished death, and brought life and immortality to light through the Gospel" (II Tim. 1:10b). He now says: "Because I live, ye shall live also" (John 14:19). The Apostle John writes: "Blessed and holy is he that hath part in the first resurrection: over these the second death *hath no power*" (Rev. 20:6a; cf. I Thess. 4:16-18).

Those who put their trust in Jesus for salvation, repent of their sins, and are baptized into Him are saved (Mk. 16:16; Acts 2:38). If they continue faithful to the end (Rev. 2:10), they will be granted "entrance into the eternal Kingdom of our Lord and Saviour Jesus Christ" (II Peter 1:11). The Christian does not need to fear hell, for in Jesus he is safe evermore!

REVIEW QUESTIONS—HELL

Fill in the Blanks:

1. Write the meaning for these words:

    a. Shoel _____

    b. Hades _____

    c. Tartarus _____

2. Explain why Jesus chose the "Valley of Hinnom" as the name for Hell.

    _____

    _____

    _____

3. List the two main descriptions of Hell. (b) Why these two?

    _____

    _____

    (b) _____

    _____

4. Give three reasons for believing in hell as a real place.

    a. _____

    b. _____

    c. _____

5. List two scriptures that reach that hell is eternal.

    a. _____; b. _____

VI

THE TWO COVENANTS

I. God's Covenants with His People.
   A. The Covenant with Noah.
   B. The Covenant with Abraham.
   C. The Sinai Covenant with Israel.
   D. The New Covenant or Christian Age.

II. The Old Testament Covenant—Sinai.
   A. History.
   B. Purpose.
   C. Duration.

III. What was Abolished on the Cross?
   A. Temporary Laws and Ceremonies, Not Basic Principles.
   B. Nine of the Ten Commandments Included in the Christian Covenant.

IV. The New Covenant Established.

V. The New Covenant Superior to the Old Covenant.
   A. A superior mediator.
   B. A superior priesthood.
   C. A superior sacrifice.
   D. A superior Covenant in that it includes the whole World.
   E. In all ways the New is a better covenant.

THE TWO COVENANTS

Throughout history God has dealt with man in various ways in different ages. These periods of time are sometimes called dispensations.

For example, the period from Adam to Moses is designated

58

the Patriarchal Age. The Word Patriarchal is derived from Latin and means "rule of the fathers." During this time, God dealt directly with men such as Noah, Abraham, and others. Revelation of God's will was rather dim, and his requirements were few. This is called the "Starlight Age" of God's revelation to man.

The second period of history is called the Mosaic Age or dispensation and extends from Moses to Christ. God revealed His will for the Israelites through the law of Moses given at Mt. Sinai. Revelation was clearer, and God's requirements were higher and more specific. This was the "Moonlight Age" of Revelation. God dealt with Israel on a national basis.

The third period of God's dealings with man is called the Christian Age. It began on Pentecost (Acts 2), and will continue till Christ comes again. This is the "Sunlight Age" of Revelation. God is now dealing with the whole world. The revelation of God's will is bright and full—Christ being the climax of all revelation (Heb. 1:2). This is the highest and the last of God's dispensations. After this will come heaven and eternity.

I. GOD'S COVENANTS WITH HIS PEOPLE

Parallel with these ages have been certain agreements or covenants which God has made with His people in His program of redeeming man. The word "covenant" or "testament" means "agreement or contract which involves both parties in the agreement." Our English word "covenant" is derived from two Latin words, con, "together," and venio, "to come." Hence it means literally, "a coming together." The Greek word for covenant is diatheke. This word is found 33 times in the New Testament. It denotes an arrangement made by a superior for the acceptance and observance of an inferior. Our English word "contract" would express the meaning of this Greek word. The contract may be accepted or rejected by the other party, but he can not alter it. But if accepted, this covenant binds both parties by its terms. Our word "will" or "testament" expresses a similar idea.

As an illustration of this, in the covenant made with Israel at Mt. Sinai God said, "if ye will obey my voice indeed, and keep my covenant, then ye shall be my own possession from among all peoples" (Ex. 14:5). Later when Moses read God's covenant to the people they responded, "all that Jehovah hath spoken will

59

we do and be obedient" (Ex. 24:7). This made it a complete covenant—binding both parties to keep it.

Some examples of covenants God has made with His people are:

A. *The Covenant With Noah.* After the flood God made a covenant with Noah saying: "And I will establish my covenant with you; neither shall all flesh be cut off any more by the waters of the flood; neither shall there any more be a flood to destroy the earth" (Gen. 9:11). The token of this covenant was the rainbow.

B. *The Covenant with Abraham.* In Genesis 15:18 God covenanted with Abraham promising the land of Palestine to him and to his seed (cf. Gen. 17:2-8). This promise and the subsequent promise of the Messiah (Gen. 22:12-18), was made providing Abraham believed and obeyed God.

C. *The Sinai Covenant With Israel.* Three months after the children of Israel came out of Egypt God made a covenant with them and gave them the Law of Moses (Ex. 19:5-6; Ex. 20; Deut. 5). This is the main covenant of the Old Testament. This will be dealt with more fully later.

D. *The New Covenant or Christian Age.* The New Testament or new Covenant which is the final one is the climax of God's revelation. "God, having of old time spoken unto the fathers in the prophets by divers portions and in divers manners, hath at the end of these days spoken unto us in his Son, whom he appointed heir of all things, through whom also he made the worlds" (Heb. 1:1-2). A fuller discussion follows on this covenant.

II. THE OLD TESTAMENT COVENANT—SINAI

A. *History.* The story of God's covenant with Israel is recorded in Exodus 19-20, and Deuteronomy 5. Having been freed from bondage in Egypt, Moses led the children of Israel across the Red Sea and to the foot of Mt. Sinai. God then came down upon the mountain and through Moses as mediator he gave the terms of the covenant to Israel. In addition to the Ten Commandments it included various rules and regulations recorded in Leviticus, plus a blueprint of the tabernacle. This was God's will for Israel until Christ should come.

B. *Purpose.* The design or purpose of the Law was summarized by Paul when he said in Galatians 3:19: "What then is the law? It was added because of transgressions, till the seed should come to whom the promise hath been made." More specifically, God's purpose in giving the law seems to be fourfold:

1. The Law was given to Israel for the purpose of a civil government. They were a nation and needed a code of civil and political laws by which to govern themselves. This purpose is clearly seen when one studies the various regulations found in the Law (see Ex. 22:1-8; Lev. 25:23-38).

2. The Law was given to teach and convict men of sin by giving them a perfect standard of morality. Paul states in Romans 7:7: "howbeit, I had not known sin, except through the law; for I had not known coveting, except the law had said, thou shalt not covet." The law taught men what sin was and what righteousness was.

3. The Law was also given to prevent the universal spread of idolatry by preserving among men the knowledge of the one true God. When Israel departed from the worship of Jehovah, a prophet would call them back to the law of Moses. Every reformation or revival was accomplished through a return to God's law.

Through the synagogue the Jews spread the knowledge of the one true God as they taught the law to the Gentiles. This knowledge of Jehovah was a great help in spreading the Gospel after Pentecost.

4. A fourth purpose was that the Law was designed to lead men to Christ. Paul writes: "So that the law is become our tutor to bring us unto Christ, that we might be justified by faith" (Gal. 3:24). The various rites and ceremonies, types and symbols in the law of Moses were designed to teach and prepare men for Christ. For example, the sacrifice of a lamb to atone for sin was an illustration of this. John the Baptist understood this when he said of Jesus, "Behold, the Lamb of God, that taketh away the sin of the world!" (John 1:29).

C. *Duration.* The Old Testament clearly teaches that the Law of Moses was a temporary covenant. Moses predicted that he would be superceded as God's lawgiver and prophet when he said, "Jehovah thy God will raise up unto thee a prophet from

61

the midst of thee, of thy brethren, like unto me; unto him ye shall hearken" (Deut. 18:15). Jeremiah confirmed the temporary nature of the Law when he wrote, "Behold, the days come, saith Jehovah, that I will make a new covenant with the house of Israel, and with the house of Judah" (Jer. 31:31).

Jesus said: "Think not that I came to destroy the law or the prophets: I came not to destroy, but to fulfill" (Matt. 5:17). Jesus fulfilled the Law of Moses when he lived up to it and fulfilled the types concerning Himself which it contained. At His death, Paul says that Jesus took the Law of Moses "out of the way, nailing it to the Cross" (Col.2:14; cf. II Cor. 3:12-14). When Jesus, on the Cross, cried, "It is finished" (John 19:30), he obviously had in mind a number of things, one being the Law of Moses. At this time, the Old Covenant had been fulfilled and was now finished (Col. 2:14).

The writer of Hebrews is very specific when he writes: "For if that first covenant had been faultless, then would no place have been sought for a second. For finding fault with them, he saith, behold, the days come, saith the Lord, that I will make a new covenant with the house of Israel and with the house of Judah" (Heb. 8:7-8). And to settle the matter once and for all he adds: "He (Christ) taketh away the first (old), that he may establish the second (new)" (Heb. 10:9b).

III. WHAT WAS ABOLISHED ON THE CROSS?

What do the Scriptures mean when they speak of the old law being nailed to the cross? The entire old law including the Ten Commandments, or only the ceremonial laws and those commands peculiar to the Mosaic Law?

A. *Temporary Laws and Ceremonies, Not Basic Principles.* The Bible is obviously not speaking of the moral principles contained in the Decalogue being abolished since to kill, steal, or lie is as sinful today as in the time of Moses. Basic moral principles of God's Kingdom have always been in effect. It was wrong to murder under the Patriarchal Age, as well as the Mosaic and Christian Ages. Basic principles do not change, but temporary laws and ceremonies belonging only to one covenant may.

Some examples of these temporary laws were: the dietary

62

laws of Leviticus, the animal sacrifices, the tabernacle and temple, the annual feasts, etc. These were nailed to the Cross.

The Sabbath day should be included in this list even though it is one of the Ten Commandments. We suggest three reasons for believing this: (1) There is no evidence in the Old Testament that the Sabbath was observed by God's people until Israel crossed the Red Sea and entered the wilderness of Sin (Ex. 16:23). The Sabbath was pronounced holy at the creation (Gen. 2:3), but this is the first mention of it being kept. (2) Sabbath observance was required of Israel to commemorate their deliverance from Egypt (Deut. 5:15). This has no direct significance to the Christian today. The Lord's Day, however, is rich in meaning to the Christian since it commemorates the Lord's Resurrection. (3) In all the places where the Ten Commandments are repeated in the New Testament, there is no mention of the Fourth Commandment concerning the Sabbath (Matt. 19:19; Luke 18:20; Rom. 13:9).

B. *Nine of the Ten Commandments Included in the Christian Covenant.* In further proof that the basic principles of God's Law are still in force, the following chart will show that nine of the ten commandments were included in the New Covenant. This makes them binding on Christians today. The one exception is the Fourth Commandment which neither Jesus nor the Apostles ever required for us today.

The Ten Commandments	*Reaffirmed In The New Testament*
1. "Thou shalt have no other gods before me" (Ex. 20:3).	1. "To us there is but one God, the Father . . . and one Lord Jesus Christ" (I Cor. 8:6).
2. "Thou shalt not make unto thee any graven image . . ." (Ex. 20:4-6).	2. Little children, keep yourselves from idols" (I John 5:21; cf. Rom. 1:23).
3. "Thou shalt not take the name of the Lord thy God in vain . . ." (Ex. 20:7).	3. "Hallowed be thy name" (Matt. 6:9; cf. I Tim. 6:1).

63

5. "Honour thy father and thy mother . . ." (Ex. 20:12).

5. "Honour thy father and mother; which is the first commandment with promise . . ." (Eph. 6:2, 3).

6. "Thou shalt not kill" (Ex. 20:13).

6. "Whosoever hateth his brother is a murderer" (I John 3:15).

7. "Thou shalt not commit adultery" (Ex. 20:14).

7. "For this thou shalt not commit adultery . . ." (Rom. 13:9; cf. Gal. 5:19-21).

8. "Thou shalt not steal" (Ex. 20:15).

8. "Let him that stole steal no more" (Eph. 4:28).

9. "Thou shalt not bear false witness" (Rom. 13:9).

9. "Thou shalt not bear false witness against thy neighbour" (Ex. 20:16).

10. "Thou shalt not covet . . ." (Ex. 20:17).

10. "Thou shalt not covet" (Rom. 13:19; cf. Heb. 13:5).

In contrast to the above, we find that the ceremonial laws were not included in the new Covenant, and, therefore, are not binding on Christians today. They belonged distinctly to the Law of Moses, and were not continued in the Christian Dispensation. Today we live under Christ and His grace and not under the Laws of Moses (John 1:17; Eph. 2:8; Rom. 6:14).

IV. THE NEW COVENANT ESTABLISHED

The New Covenant was predicted not only by Jeremiah (Jer. 31:31) but also by Isaiah: "And it shall come to pass in the latter days, that the mountain of Jehovah's house shall be established on the top of the mountain, and shall be exalted above the hills; and all nations shall flow into it . . . and He will teach us of his ways, and we will walk in his paths; for out of Zion shall go forth the law, and the Word of Jehovah from Jerusalem" (Isa. 2:2-3). This New Covenant unlike the old, would include "all nations" (Isa. 2:2), not just Israel. It would be written on the hearts of men and not on tables of stone (Jer. 31:31; Ex. 24:12). It would come to pass in the latter days or "last days" (Isa. 2:2; Acts 2:17). This refers to the Christian Age. The New Covenant would begin in Jerusalem and the Word of God would go forth from there (Isa. 2:3; Luke 24:46-47).

Isaiah 2:2-3 was fulfilled on Pentecost, 30 A.D., in Jerusalem. Seven weeks before this Jesus had nailed the Law to His Cross after having fulfilled it. Now, on the day of Pentecost, Jesus sends the Holy Spirit from heaven and baptizes the apostles. Peter preached the first full gospel message which is recorded in Acts 2. Three thousand Jews believed his message and in repentance obeyed the gospel in baptism. This was the beginning of the Church of Christ, and the New Covenant was officially inaugurated. This Covenant will continue until superceded by the "eternal Kingdom of Our Lord and Saviour Jesus Christ" (II Pet. 1:11).

V. THE NEW COVENANT SUPERIOR TO THE OLD COVENANT

In order to understand why God replaced the Old Covenant with the New, let us look at some of the differences and the superiority of the New Covenant to the Old.

A. *A superior mediator.* Old Law—Moses was the principal mediator of the old law (Deut. 5:4-5; Ex. 31:18; Jn. 1:17). New Law—Christ is the mediator of the New Covenant (Jn. 1:17; I Tim. 2:5). The Old Covenant had a human mediator; the New has a divine mediator.

B. *A superior priesthood.* Old Covenant—Under the Old Covenant the high priest was Aaron—a human high priest (Ex. 28:1). Succeding high priests were descendants of Aaron—also human priests.

Since they were human priests they had sins like all men (Ex. 32:1-6; 32:21-24; Lev. 10:1-2). Aaron was reminded of this frailty on the Day of Atonement when he was required to take the blood of the bullock and sprinkle it upon the mercy seat first. This was to make atonement for himself and for his house (Lev. 16:11-14). Afterward, he sprinkled the blood of the goat on the mercy seat for the sins of Israel (Lev. 16:15; 9:7).

New Covenant—Jesus is now our divine high priest (Heb. 4:14-16). Christ being "holy, guileless, undefiled, separated from sinners, and made higher than the heavens . . . needeth not daily, like those high priests, to offer up sacrifices, first for his own sins, and then for the sins of the people: for this he did once for all, when he offered up himself" (Heb. 7:26-27).

Another superiority is that Aaron continued to offer the sacrifice for atonement each year. Christ, however, offered a sacrifice for sin—Himself—only once to obtain complete atonement for sin (Heb. 9:26).

C. *A superior sacrifice*. Old Covenant—Under the old law the sacrifice was that of the blood of bulls and goats. This atonement was made annually (Ex. 30: 10; Heb. 9:25). We understand now that these sacrifices did not completely take away sin but simply rolled them forward until Christ should die. Hebrews says, "But in those sacrifices there is a remembrance made of sins year by year. For it is impossible that the blood of bulls and goats should take away sins" (Heb. 10:3-4). These sacrifices for sin were incomplete without the sacrifice of Christ on the Cross.

New Covenant—The blood of Christ, God's Son, was the full, complete, and eternal sacrifice for sins. "But Christ having come a high priest of the good things to come, through the greater and more perfect tabernacle, not made with hands, that is to say, not of this creation. Nor yet through he blood of goats and calves, but through his own blood, entered in once for all into the holy place, having obtained eternal redemption" (Heb. 9:11-12). It was a superior sacrifice with superior efficacy.

D. *A superior Covenant in that it includes the whole world*. The Sinai Covenant was made between God and Israel alone (Ex. 34:27). "And Jehovah said unto Moses, Write thou these words: for after the tenor of these words I have made a covenant with thee and with Israel." God's covenant in the Christian Age is with the whole world (Matt. 28:18-20; Mark 16:15; Acts 1:8; Acts 2:30). There are no racial barriers; there are no geographical barriers (Acts 10:34-35); Rom. 1:14; Gal. 3:28-29). Of course, only those who comply with the terms of admission to the Kingdom are in a covenant relationship with Christ. The terms of admission into the New Covenant are faith, or trust in Christ, repentance for sin, and baptism into Christ (Mark 16:15-16; Acts 2:28).

E. *In all ways the New is a better covenant.* However one looks at the Gospel or the New Covenant it is superior to the Old. The message of the book of Hebrews is the superiority of Christ and Christianity, over the Old Law and Judaism. The key word of the epistle is "better." It occurs 13 times. The New Covenant has:

a. better revelation (Heb. 1:1-4).
b. better hope (Heb. 7:19).
c. better priesthood (Heb. 7:20-28).
d. better promises (Heb. 8:6).
e. better covenant (Heb. 8:6; 7:22).
f. better sacrifice (Heb. 9:23).
g. better possession (Heb. 10:34).
h. better country (heaven) (Heb. 11:16).
i. better resurrection (Heb. 11:35).

To say as the New Testament does that the Law was imperfect or faulty (Heb. 8:8) in no way reflects on the value and importance of the Law of Moses.

It was perfect for the purpose for which it was given. Paul says in Romans 7:12: "So that the Law is holy, and the commandment holy, and righteous, and good." Jesus echoed this sentiment when he said: "Till Heaven and earth pass away, one jot or one tittle shall in no wise pass away from the law, till all things be accomplished" (Matt. 5:18).

The Law was never designed to save man (Gal. 3:11). It was given for the purposes listed earlier in this chapter. When the Law had fulfilled its divine purpose, it was replaced by the Gospel which *is* "the power of God unto salvation to everyone that believeth" (Rom. 1:16).

REVIEW QUESTIONS—TWO COVENANTS

Fill in the Blanks:

1. List the three dispensations or ages found in the Bible.

    a. _____

    b. _____

    c. _____

2. Covenant means: _____

    _____

3. List three purposes for the old covenant.

    a. _____

    b. _____

    c. _____

4. What part of the Law was nailed to the cross when Christ died?

    _____

    _____

5. In what ways is the New Covenant superior to the Old?

    a. _____

    b. _____

    c. _____

THE EVIDENCE OF PARDON

VII

THE EVIDENCE OF PARDON

I. THE NATURE AND IMPORTANCE OF THIS SUBJECT

This lesson is concerned with answering these questions: How may one have assurance that his sins have been pardoned? How can we know that we are children of God? How can a Christian know that he is continuing in Christ or in a saved relationship to Christ?

69

Surely these are vital and practical questions and their importance cannot be over emphasized. Jesus told His apostles by implication that one soul is worth more than the whole world. He asked the question "For what is a man profited, if he shall gain the whole world, and· lose his own soul?" (Matt. 16:26-KJV). The salvation of one's soul is the most important concern in any man's life. Peter urged the brethren in his day to "give the more diligence to make your calling and election sure" (II Peter 1:10a).

A wise man will not risk a false answer or even a doubtful one to the question, "What must I do to be saved?" He will make sure! The purpose of this lesson is to search the Scriptures and find the *sure* answer to this question.

II.   THE ASSURANCE OF NEW TESTAMENT WRITERS ON THIS POINT

It is God's *will that man should have a clear* answer to this question of salvation and that his life be characterized by a quiet assurance on this point. Isaiah speaking of the reign of the Messiah wrote, "And the work of righteousness shall be peace; and the effect of righteousness *quietness* and *assurance* for ever" (Isa. 32:17-KJV).

This quiet assurance of salvation is obvious to any reader of the New Testament. "We *know* that we have passed out of death into life, because we love the brethren" (I John 3:14). "Beloved, *now are we children of God*" (I John 3:2a). "And *being made free from sin*, ye became servants of righteousness" (Rom. 6:18). "For *I know him whom I have believed*, and I am persuaded that he is able to guard that which I have committed unto him against that day" (II Tim. 1:12b). There is no uncertain note in these declarations of faith but only conviction and assurance.

Paul wrote "how that our gospel came not unto you in word only, but also in power, and in the Holy Spirit, and *in much assurance*" (I Thess. 1:5). Speaking of Christ's resurrection, Luke writes "to whom he also showed himself alive after his passion by *many proofs*, appearing unto them by the space of forty days, and speaking the things concerning the kingdom of God" (Acts 1:3). Colossians 2:2 speaks of "full assurance of

70

understanding"; Hebrews 6:11 of "full assurance of hope"; and Hebrews 10:22 of the "full assurance of faith."

This assurance was not a formal acceptance of some doctrine but it was a vital certainty incorporated into the very life of the Christian.

III. CONTRAST THE UNCERTAINTY OF MANY CHRISTIANS TODAY

Unfortunately, many Christians do not exhibit the same confidence today that is seen in the New Testament. Too often there is a vagueness and uncertainty regarding the matter of their salvation. If you ask some people "Are you a Christian?" They will answer "I hope so. I'm trying to be," or some equally indefinite answer. The attitude expressed is like the song which says:

"Tis a point I long to know,
And oft it causes anxious thought:
Do I love the Lord or no?
Am I His or am I not?"[1]

If one were to ask a man "Are you married?" He would not reply "I hope so! I'm trying to be!" He would know whether he was married or not. There are certain requirements to be met when a man and woman become married and they know whether they have complied with these requirements.

In like manner there are certain conditions to be met when one is married to Christ. A Christian can know if he has complied with these conditions and, therefore, should be able to speak with confidence. Dr. C.C. Crawford writes:

It seems to me that we should be able to know, and indeed should know, whether or not our sins have been pardoned, whether or not we have been adopted into God's Household (made members of Christ's Body and citizens of His kingdom), with a knowledge (certitude) that is not based on speculation or theory, but on reliable evidence (fact). This is what is meant by the title, "The Evidence of Pardon."[1]

[1]Crawford, C.C., Sermon Outlines on First Principles, (Dehoff Publications, 1961), p. 185.
[1]Crawford, C.C., Sermon Outlines on First Principles, (Dehoff Publications, 1961), p. 185.

71

IV. SOME SOURCES THAT DO NOT PROVIDE ADE-QUATE EVIDENCE OF PARDON

A. *A Special Communication from God.* Many people expect Christ to speak to them today as He did to the paralytic lowered through the roof: "Son, be of good cheer; thy sins are forgiven" (Matt. 9:2b); or the dying thief when He said, "Today shall thou be with me in Paradise" (Luke 23:43). They seem to expect God to make them an exception and speak from Heaven a personal message relating to their salvation.

Many people trust in lights, visions, or voices to assure them that they are saved. On one occasion the author visited a lady 91 years old. When he spoke to her concerning the salvation of her soul she replied: "Son, do not worry about me for I am all right. I know I am saved." Since she had not obeyed the Gospel, I asked her on what she based this conviction. She replied: "Last night I was lying in my bed and suddenly the room was filled with light. Do you know what that light meant?" I replied that I did not. She said, "That light was the Lord telling me that I was saved and that I am ready to meet Him." No amount of reasoning from the Scriptures as to Christ's requirements for salvation affected her in the least. She died believing that that light was God's assurance to her of salvation.

The Apostle Peter stated that Jesus in "His Divine power *hath* granted unto us *all things* that pertain unto *life* and *godliness*" (II Peter 1:3). The tense of the verb "hath given" is past tense. Jesus has already given it. Nearly 2,000 years ago Jesus gave *in His word* all the things that we need to attain forgiveness and to live a godly life. He has not promised to make a special revelation for each person coming to Him. He has certainly given that communication to us in His word.

Why expect a new revelation? It is as unreasonable as to expect a special telegram to confirm a well-attested letter from a friend. If you will not believe his letter, what evidence has he that you will believe his telegram? If we will not believe the word of God in the Bible, why would we believe a special message from the same source?[1]

"The minute we deviate from the Scripture doctrine of the

---

[1]Davis, M. M., *First Principles,* (The Standard Publishing Company, 1904), p. 188.

all-sufficiency of the Gospel as the means used by the Holy Spirit to effect the conversion of sinners, just that moment do we begin to lose ourselves in the jungles of speculation, mysticism, and all kinds of fanaticism. The true evidence of pardon is not to be obtained from any special revelation."[2]

B. *A special kind of feeling.* Some people rely upon some special feeling, a mysterious ecstasy of some kind for their assurance of pardon. Feelings are induced by testimony and, therefore, are only as reliable as the testimony is factual.

This fact is well illustrated by an incident connected with the famous Battle of Waterloo on June 18, 1815. The Duke of Wellington was engaged in the crucial battle with Napoleon Bonaparte. All England waited with great apprehension for word from the battle. Just before dark of that eventful day, the signal flashed across the English Channel these words: "Wellington defeated." At that moment the fog moved in and the remainder of the message was lost. Fear and consternation reigned in England that night. The next morning when the fog lifted the full message came through: "Wellington defeated Napoleon." Rejoicing now filled the land.

Feelings can be deceptive and undependable unless produced by facts. There must be a sure foundation of facts on which to rest one's salvation.

Multitudes rest this great matter on the frail basis of fleshly feelings. If they feel good, they are forgiven; if they feel bad, they are unforgiven. They forget that feelings are largely dependent on health, the weather, our surroundings, etc. But salvation is independent of all these. We may be saved in health or in sickness; in good weather or bad; and in spite of surroundings. They forget, also, that feelings are deceptive. As Jacob listened to the false reports of his sinful boys, and looked upon the bloody coat of Joseph, he felt that his child was dead. But his feelings deceived him. They seem not to understand that feelings are an *effect,* and not a *cause.* God forgives. This is a *cause.* The forgiven soul is happy. This is the *result.* We do not know we are forgiven because

---

[2]Crawford, C. C., *Sermon Outlines on First Principles,* (Dehoff Publications, 1961), p. 190-191.

we are happy, but we are happy because we know we are forgiven.[1]

People vary greatly in their emotional reactions. This is why it is unwise to depend on feelings for evidence of salvation. There would always be doubt as to which feeling was the proper one. As W. H. Book has written:

I do not believe that all people in conversion have identically the same experience. We are not all constituted alike.

We see a river overflowing its banks, which was caused by a mighty flood. There has been a great storm—the lighting flashed—the thunder roared—the winds blew. The water came down in torrents. The river channel was full to overflowing.

I behold in another locality a river which has also overflowed its banks; but there has been no thunder—no flashing of the lighting—no roaring of the winds. No rain has been seen to fall. What has caused this flood? Go up on the mountain-side. The snow, under the powerful influence of the sun, has melted, run down the mountain-sides into the river channel, and quietly and gently and noiselessly has filled it to the brim. Two rivers, both full—full to overflowing—and yet under different circumstances!

Here is a man in the congregation, a sinner. He is emotional; easily moved. Under the spell of the gospel he gives vent to his feelings, shouts, rejoices. His heart has been filled; his life is full of the grace of God. Sitting by his side is another man, a sinner, of a quiet nature; not one bit emotional—logical, thoughtful. He has listened to the gospel, too. It has impressed him. He comes forward, makes his confession, obeys its commands, and rejoices, but not with the same demonstration. Both have been converted. The hearts of both are full.[1]

Nothing that has been written here is intended to minimize

[1]Davis, M. M., *First Principles*, (Standard Publishing Company, 1904), p. 188-189.
[1]Book, William Henry, *The Columbus Tabernacle Sermons*, (Standard Publishing Company, 1909), p. 129-130.

or degrade in any way the genuine feeling that comes at the time of conversion. After the jailor in Philippi believed in Christ and had been baptized, he brought Paul and Silas into his house, "and set food before them, and *rejoiced greatly,* with all his house, having believed in God" (Acts 16:34). The Ethiopian eunuch "went on his way *rejoicing,*" after Philip had baptized him (Acts 8:39). When one has obeyed the Gospel and God has forgiven him there should surge through his heart a joy and peace that passes understanding. However, to take one's feelings alone as the criteria of Divine pardon would be an unreliable evidence.

C. *Sincerity and a clear conscience as evidence of pardon.* Others rely upon sincerity and a clear conscience as evidence that God has forgiven them. Sincerity and a clear conscience both are parts of a true believer's life. But they alone do not constitute proper evidence of pardon.

Formerly in India it was believed that when the Ganges River overflowed and destroyed the crops that the god of the river was angry. To placate him a young mother might take her infant son to the banks of the swollen river and cast it in as a sacrifice to the god. If you were to ask her "How could you do such a deed? *Does not your conscience* hurt you because you have killed your child?" Her answer would have been, "No, I did this because my god required it. My conscience is clear."

Jacob was sincere when he said that his boy was dead and he would see him no more this side of the grave. Paul was as sincere when persecuting the church as he was later, when he defended it, and gave his life as a sacrifice for Christ. Can you not recall cases in your own life, and in the lives of your friends, in which you were sincerely in the wrong? This fine element of character—sincerity—is found alike in the bosoms of those whose causes are just, and those whose causes are unjust, and hence it proves only the moral integrity of the man, and not the righteousness of his cause. A cruel illustration of this thought took place recently in one of our state prisons. The boy was not very bright, and some of his fellow-prisoners brought him what he thought was a regular pardon from the Governor. He believed it was genuine, and he leaped and danced for joy, and stood at the door watching for an officer to come and lead him out. He was as happy as if it had been true, but his happiness did not last. His feelings deceived him.[1]

One's conscience is reliable only to the extent that it is taught the true facts. Sincerity is an excellent quality but unless one has the facts he can be sincerely wrong. These alone are inadequate evidences of salvation.

V. THE PROPER EVIDENCE OF PARDON

A. *Some comments on forgiveness. Forgiveness takes place in the mind of God.* Before examining the proper evidences of forgiveness, it is well to note some facts concerning forgiveness. C. C. Crawford writes: "pardon is not something done within us, but something done in heaven for us."[2] A pardon is issued from the seat of government by one who has the authority to issue a pardon. In spiritual matters, forgiveness takes place in the mind of God since he is the one who forgives our sins.

We can only know we are pardoned when God tells us. If one has offended a friend and then asks for forgiveness, he can only know that he is forgiven when the friend says, "I forgive you." The same is true of God. We can only be sure that we are forgiven when He tells us when and on what conditions He will forgive us.

God alone has the power or authority to set the terms upon which He will forgive us. Since He is the one who has been sinned against and is the proper one to forgive us, then He has the right to state on what basis He will forgive sins. Our task is to find what those terms of forgiveness are and then do them.

B. *The terms of forgiveness are set forth in God's Word.* The Bible clearly teaches what the terms of pardon are. It also teaches that obedience to this revealed Word is imperative for forgiveness. Paul writes: "But thanks be to God, that, whereas ye were servants of sin, ye became obedient from the heart to that form of teaching where unto ye were delivered; and being made

---

[1]Davis, M. M., *How to Be Saved,* (Standard Publishing Company, Cincinnati), p. 203.

[2]Crawford, C. C., *Sermon Outlines on First Principles,* (Dehoff Publications, 1961), p. 194.

free from sin, ye became servants of righteousness" (Rom. 6:17-18). One is made free from sin by obeying the doctrine which is the Gospel. Peter writes: "Seeing ye have purified your souls in *obeying the truth* through the Spirit . . ." (I Peter 1:22-KJV). Souls are purified by obeying the truth revealed by the Spirit. Jesus said: "Not everyone that saith unto me Lord, Lord, shall enter the Kingdom of Heaven; but he that *doeth the will of my Father* who is in heaven" (Matt. 7:21).

The sure evidence of pardon or forgiveness is to be found in the clear statements of God's word. To "the law and to the testimony," we must go for the certain answer to the question, "What must I do to be saved?" (Isa. 8:20; Luke 16:20; John 8:31-32; John 17:17).

C. *The two witnesses who bear testimony to our salvation.* Paul writes in Romans 8:16 that "the Spirit himself beareth witness with our spirit, that we are children of God." Deuteronomy 19:15 states that it takes two or more witnesses to establish any fact. Paul states that we have two witnesses to our salvation—the Holy Spirit and our own spirit. When these two agree, we have the assurance of forgiveness that we seek.

How does this work? It works like this: God's Spirit reveals in the Word what one must do to be saved. When one's spirit tells him that he has done these things, then he has the two-fold witness which establishes the fact.

What does the Spirit reveal as God's terms of pardon? Here they are:

1. God's Spirit tells us that we must believe that Jesus is our Saviour and God's Son in order to be saved (Mark 16:16; John 20:30-31; Acts 16:31). The believer's spirit tells him that he *does* believe these great facts concerning Jesus.

2. God's Spirit tells us that we must repent of all sin in order to be saved (Acts 2:38; Luke 24:46-47). The believer's spirit tells him that he has repented of all sin. A man might deceive the world about his repentance but he can not deceive the Spirit of God nor can he deceive *his own spirit.*

3. God's Spirit tells us that we must confess Christ before men in order to be forgiven (Matt. 10:32-33; Rom. 10:9-10). The believer's spirit tells him that he has sincerely confessed his faith in Christ.

4. God's Spirit tells us that we must be buried with the Lord in baptism and raised up to a new life in order to be saved (Acts 2:38; Gal. 3:27; Rom. 6:1-7). The believer's spirit tells him that he has sincerely obeyed this command of Jesus.

Thus God's Spirit in testifying as to the terms of pardon under the New Covenant, and our spirits in testifying that we have complied with those terms, agree upon one and the same fact, namely that we are children of God, heirs of God and joint-heirs with Christ (Rom. 8:14-17). Nothing could be plainer, and so our text asserts. Our evidence of pardon consists not in such ephemeral things as dreams, visions, trances, ecstasies, and like psychic phenomena, but in the sure foundation of God Almighty's word (Matt. 24:35). And so we sing:

> How firm a foundation, ye saints of the Lord,
> Is laid for your faith, in His excellent word!
> What more can He say than to you He hath said,
> You who unto Jesus for refuge have fled?[1]

D. *This principle illustrated.* The following illustration will serve to clarify and we trust to convince the reader concerning our entire argument:

A man is in the penitentiary. His friends petition the governor, and he is pardoned on certain conditions. With a happy heart he starts to his home. The sheriff of his county, not knowing of his pardon, meets him on the highway, and commands him to halt. "Why do you halt me?" says the man. "I have been pardoned." "What evidence can you give of your pardon?" answers the sheriff. "Well, Mr. Sheriff," says the man, "it is a strange story I have to tell, but it is true. Last night about twelve o'clock, when all was dark and still in my cell, suddenly a light brighter than yonder sun shone about me, and I heard a voice saying, 'John Smith, you are a pardoned man.'" The sheriff cooly responds: "I've no doubt you think you saw and heard all this, and doubtless it would

---

[1]Crawford, C. C., *Sermon Outlines on First Principles,* (Dehoff Publications, 1961), p. 193-194.

be all right in religious circles, but it is a little too fanciful for the courts of Caesar, and you may consider yourself under arrest." But the man, laying his hand on his heart, continues, "Mr. Sheriff, I *feel* that I am pardoned." "I do not question your feelings," answers the sensible but not over-sentimental sheriff, "but feelings, like visions and voices, are not good evidence in our courts," and he is about to proceed with his prisoner to the jail. "Hold, Mr. Sheriff!" cries the man with much vehemence, "I declare to you that I am *thoroughly honest* and sincere!" "That may be true," replies the officer, "but like everything else you've said, it is unsatisfactory as evidence in our courts, and therefore it is my duty to arrest you" and his stern face indicates business, when the ex-convict pulls from his pocket a paper, saying' "Here is evidence which I know you'll accept." And it proves to be a pardon from Governor Lanham, of Texas, bearing the seal of the state, in which the man is pardoned *provided* that on or before 1 p.m. of Dec. 1, 1903, he leaves the State, and never more returns. "This is all right," says the sheriff. "Why did you not show it at first and save all this trouble?"

At 12:30 p.m., December 1, he crosses the Rio Grande River at El Paso, and takes up his abode in Mexico. You meet him an hour later, and ask him if he has been pardoned. What would he say? Would he answer that he thought so? He hoped so? He felt so? Certainly not. His answer would be prompt, clear and positive. He would say, "Yes."

And then, if you should ask for the evidence on which he based this confident answer, he would tell you that Governor Lanham promised him pardon on certain conditions of pardon, and the spirit of the man assures him that he had faithfully observed them; and therefore he had the highest possible evidence of forgiveness. Let the Governor represent God, and the pardoned man the sinner, and we have not only a true picture of this important principle, but one so simple that all can understand.[1]

---

[1]Davis, M. M., *First Principles*, (Standard Publishing Company, 1904), p. 192-194.

79

VI.   CONTINUING EVIDENCE OF ONE'S SALVATION

Not only does God want us to be assured of our forgiveness of the past, but He also wants us to rest confidently in His love daily. The Scriptures do not teach once in grace always in grace. But, there are certain evidences whereby one can be assured of continuing salvation. John assures us: "These things have I written unto you that believe on the name of the Son of God; that ye may know that ye have eternal life" (I John 5:13-KJV). Here are three guideposts by which we may have assurance that we continue in a saved relationship with God:

A.   *By keeping the commandments of Christ.* Only by being faithful to Him can one be assured of salvation. John writes: "And hereby we know that we know him, if we keep his commandments. He that saith, I know him, and keepeth not his commandments, is a liar, and the truth is not in him; but whoso keepeth his word, in him verily hath the love of God been perfected. Hereby we know that we are in him" (I John 2:3-5; cf. I John 2:15-17; James 4:4). Jesus speaks to the church in Smyrna "be thou faithful unto death and I will give thee the crown of life" (Rev. 2:10b).

B.   *Love for the brethren—a sign of salvation.* "We know that we have passed out of death into life, because we love the brethren" (I John 3:14a). "My little children, let us not love in word, neither with the tongue; but in deed and truth. Hereby shall we know that we are of the truth, and shall assure our heart before Him" (I John 3:18-19).

C.   *The indwelling presence of the Holy Spirit gives assurance of salvation.* "Hereby we know that we abide in him and he in us, because he hath given us of his Spirit" (I John 4:13). "And hereby we know that he abideth in us, by the Spirit which he gave us" (I John 3:24b).

Salvation, forgiveness, pardon are found "in Christ." The terms of pardon brings us into Christ (Gal. 3:26-27). Remaining faithful *keeps us in Christ* (Rev. 2:10b; I John 3:24a). John simply and clearly summarizes this grand thought when he writes: "He that hath the Son hath the life; he that hath not the Son of God hath not the life" (I John 5:12).

VII. ETERNAL SALVATION

Jesus said that the way to remain saved for all eternity is to be faithful to Him. "Be thou faithful unto death, and I will give thee the crown of life" (Rev. 2:10b).

Paul echoed these words when he wrote: "I have fought the good fight, I have finished the course, *I have kept the faith:* henceforth there is laid up for me the crown of righteousness, which the Lord, the righteous judge, shall give to me at that day; and not to me only, but also to all them that have loved his appearing" (II Tim. 4:7-8). Before he could receive the crown he had to keep the faith and complete the course.

Peter expressed a similar idea when he wrote that the Christian is to continue to add to his life the graces of temperance, patience, brotherly kindness, love, etc. "For if ye do these things, ye shall never stumble: for thus shall be richly supplied unto you the entrance into the eternal kingdom of our Lord and Saviour Jesus Christ" (II Peter 1:10b-11).

God has provided all the power we need to be saved from the past, to remain saved in the present, and to be eternally saved in the future. This is provided through Christ and the Gospel. But, we must remain in Christ to have this full assurance of eternal salvation.

REVIEW QUESTIONS—THE EVIDENCE OF PARDON

1. List three unreliable evidences of pardon.

   a. _____

   b. _____

   c. _____

2. Why are feelings alone unreliable as evidence of salvation?

   _____

   _____

   _____

3. What are the two witnesses to one's salvation?

   a. _____   b. _____

4. Why is basing one's salvation on the Word of God more sure than the other sources of evidence?

   _____

   _____

   _____

5. What evidence does the Christian have of continuing salvation?

   a. _____

   b. _____

   c. _____

VIII
THE PERSON AND GIFT OF THE HOLY SPIRIT

I. The Person of the Holy Spirit.
   A. Mistaken ideas about the Holy Spirit.
   B. The Holy Spirit is a Person.

II. The Gift of the Holy Spirit.
   A. What is the "Gift of the Holy Spirit"?
   B. Evidence for this explanation.
   C. How does the Christian know the
      Holy Spirit dwells within?

III. Blessings the Holy Spirit Brings.
   A. He enables the Christian to
      bear fruits of righteousness.
   B. He brings power to help the
      Christian overcome sin.
   C. The Holy Spirit seals the Christian.
   D. He intercedes for the Christian and
      provides power for prayer.
   E. The Spirit sustains the Christian in hope.
   F. The presence of the Spirit assures the
      believer's resurrection.

IV. Our Obligation or Response To The Indwelling Spirit.
   A. Not to grieve the Spirit.
   B. We are not to quench the Spirit.
   C. We are to walk by the Spirit.

THE PERSON AND GIFT OF THE HOLY SPIRIT

The Person and work of the Holy Spirit is a neglected study in many churches. Some Christians think that the subject is so deep and mysterious that it is futile to study it. Others hesitate to emphasize the study of the Holy Spirit since some religious groups hold such extreme views regarding Him. Still it is encouraging to see many Christians making a serious study of the Bible teaching on the Holy Spirit.

The New Testament leaves no doubt as to the importance of the Holy Spirit to the Christian's life. Paul writes: "But if any man hath not the Spirit of Christ, he is none of his" (Rom. 8:9b). John adds: "Hereby we known that we abide in him and he in us, because he hath given us of his Spirit" (I John 4:13).

The Holy Spirit then is the special Helper sent to carry on Jesus' work, and to live in the Christian. His presence assures the Christian of his salvation and that he belongs to God. This is important!

I. THE PERSON OF THE HOLY SPIRIT

A. *Mistaken ideas about the Holy Spirit.*

1. The Holy Spirit is an emotion. The study of the Holy Spirit is encumbered with many mistaken ideas. Some think of the Holy Spirit only as an emotion. Some will tap themselves on their chests and say, "I can feel the Holy Spirit in my heart." If the service is lively and stirs the emotions, the Spirit is said to surely be present. But if the worship does not stir the emotions, that is a sure sign that the Spirit is not present.

The Holy Spirit does bring joy and peace to the believer. He does stir the emotions; but He is far more than an emotion.

2. Others view the Holy Spirit merely as a divine influence. They think He is not a distinct person, but a good influence coming from God and Jesus.

3. Still others have identified Him with the Word of God—the Bible. Because the New Testament states that the Holy Spirit does certain things and later it says the Word does them, some have concluded that they are one and the same. For example, Jesus said we are "born" of the Holy Spirit (Jn. 3:3-8): Peter declares that we are "begotten . . . through the word of God" (I Pet. 1:23-25).

Here are other examples of actions that both the Holy Spirit and the Word are said to do: (a) Give life (II Cor. 3:6; James 1:18); (b) Create (Gen. 1:2; Job 33:4; Heb. 11:3; II Pet. 3:5); (c) Save (Tit. 3:5; James 1:21); (d) Sanctify (II Thess. 2:13; I Cor. 6:11; Jn. 17:17); and (e) Dwell within (Rom. 8:11; Col. 3:16).

The Holy Spirit and the Word of God are inseparable in

their actions. This is because the Word is the "Sword of the Spirit" (Eph. 6:17). It is the instrument through which He works. But we should not mistake the instrument for the agent. The gun is not identical with the soldier, nor the hammer with the carpenter. The Holy Spirit is the agent of all these things, and the Word is the instrument He uses. The Holy Spirit and the Word of God are inseparable but not identical.

B. *The Holy Spirit is a Person.* The Bible teaches that the Holy Spirit is a Person. A person is a being who is conscious of self, endowed with the ability to think and reason; who has feeling or emotions, and who has a free will and able to take responsible action. The Holy Spirit is said to possess all these qualities. Here are three proofs that He is a Person:

1. He is said to do what only persons can do.
   (a) He speaks. (I Tim. 4:1; Rev. 2:7)
   (b) He testifies. (John 15:26)
   (c) He teaches. (John 14:26; I Cor. 2:13)
   (d) He leads and forbids. (Acts 16:6, 7)
2. He is said to have characteristics of a person.
   (a) Mind. (Rom. 8:27)
   (b) Affection, or love. (Rom. 15:30)
   (c) Will. (I Cor. 12:11)
   (d) Being grieved or vexed. (Isa. 63:10; Eph. 4:30)
   (e) Being resisted. (Acts 7:51)
   (f) Being sinned against. (Matt. 12:24-32)
3. Personal pronouns in the masculine gender are applied to the Holy Spirit. The noun "spirit" is neuter in gender. Normally all its pronouns and modifiers would be neuter. But in the New Testament all pronouns referring to the Holy Spirit are masculine. A good illustration of this is John 16:13 "Howbeit when *he,* the Spirit of truth, is come, *he* shall guide you into all the truth; for *he* shall not speak from *himself;* but what things soever *he* shall hear, these shall *he* speak; and *he* shall declare unto you the things that are to come."

There are seven masculine, personal pronouns in this one verse. The Holy Spirit should not be referred to as "it," a nonentity, but as "he" a living, thinking, feeling, acting person.

C. *The Holy Spirit is a Divine Person.* The Bible teaches

84

that the Holy Spirit is a Divine Person with Deity like that of God and Christ.

    1.   He has the attributes of God.

       a)   He is eternal. (Heb. 9:14); Was with God in creation. (Gen. 1:2)

       b)   Knows what God knows. (I Cor. 2:10, 11)

       c)   He exerts the power of God. (Luke 1:35; Acts 1:8; Micah 3:8; Judges 14:6)

       d)   Baptized into His name. (Matt. 28:19, 20)

       e)   He is everywhere present as God is. (Ps. 139:7-10)

       f)   He is holy, the Spirit of holiness. (Romans 1:4); Spirit of grace. (Heb. 10:29); Spirit of truth. (Jn. 14:17; 16:13); Spirit of wisdom. (Isa. 11:2)

    2.   The Spirit does work like God.

       a)   Creation. (Gen. 1:2; Job 33:4; Psa. 104:30)

       b)   Giving life. (Gen. 2:7; Rom. 8:11; Jn. 3:5; 6:63; Gal. 6:8)

       c)   Authorship of prophecies. (II Peter 1:21)

       d)   Working of miracles. (Matt. 12:28; I Cor. 12:9, 11)

II. THE GIFT OF THE HOLY SPIRIT

At the conclusion of his sermon on Pentecost, Peter told the inquiring Jews to "Repent ye, and be baptized everyone of you in the name of Jesus Christ unto (for) the remission of your sins; and ye shall receive the gift of the Holy Spirit" (Acts 2:38).

A. *What is the "Gift of the Holy Spirit"?* Some say it is the gift of salvation, which God gives to those who obey the Gospel. They hold that the last clause in Acts 2:38 is a repetition of the preceding one; in other words, the gift which the Holy Spirit gives is salvation or "remission of sins." This is a needless repetition and in view of other Scriptures is rejected as being the meaning of Peter's promise.

What then is this "gift"? It is the Holy Spirit *Himself* which is given to every baptized believer in Christ. Peter promised two gifts if they repented and were baptized—the remission of sins and the Holy Spirit as a gift. Let us examine the proof for this view.

B. *Evidence for this explanation.*

1. Jesus promised that the Holy Spirit would live within the believer. "And I will pray the Father, and he shall give you another Comforter, that he may be with you for ever, even the Spirit of truth: whom the world cannot receive: for it beholdeth him not, neither knoweth him: ye know him; for he abideth with you, and shall be in you" (Jn. 14:16-17: cf., Jn. 7:37-39).

It is clear from this Scripture that Peter repeated at Pentecost what Jesus had already promised. Jesus said that His disciples, not the world would receive the Holy Spirit. Peter promised the Holy Spirit to those cleansed from their sins.

This is also in harmony with the laws of purification in the Old Testament. When a priest was to be consecrated to the priesthood, he was taken to the laver in the outer court and washed completely. Then he was anointed with oil and clothed with the holy garments. The washing was symbolic of baptism and the inward cleansing from sin. The anointing was symbolic of the gift of the Holy Spirit (See Acts 10:38; Heb. 1:9).

2. The apostles taught the indwelling of the Holy Spirit. Peter in Acts 5:32 says, "And we are witnesses of these things; and, so is the Holy Spirit, whom God hath given to them that obey Him." Paul adds, "Know ye not that your body is a temple of the Holy Spirit which is in you, which ye have from God?" (I Cor. 6:19; cf., I Cor. 3:16; I Jn. 3:24b; Gal. 4:6). Paul further states, "Therefore he that rejecteth, rejecteth not man, but God, who giveth His Holy Spirit unto you" (I Thess. 4:8).

The marvelous truth is that not only does the Holy Spirit dwell within us, but that the Father and Son do also through the Spirit who dwells within. "If a man love me, he will keep my word: and my Father will love him, and we will come unto him, and make our abode with him" (Jn. 14:23; cf., Jn. 14:18). "As Jesus Christ is 'God with us,' so the Holy Spirit is 'God-in-Christ' with us."

C. *How does the Christian know the Holy Spirit dwells within?* This question troubles many people, especially those who rely upon emotion as the primary assurance that they have received the Spirit. Emotions are fleeting things and can deceive; one needs a stronger, surer foundation. Here are some ways we can be assured we have the Spirit of God.

1.   By faith when one obeys the Gospel. How did the people at Pentecost know they had the Spirit dwelling in them? They knew that the conditions to receive this heavenly Gift were Faith in Christ, Repentance, and Baptism into Christ for the remission of sins. They knew when they had complied with those conditions, and they believed that God would keep His promise when they did. Therefore they knew they had received the Spirit because God had promised; and they believed God. How does one know he has the remission of sins? The same way. One can be assured that when he does his part, God will do His. By Faith we accept and believe God's promise in both these great blessings.

2.   The presence of the "fruit of the Spirit" in our lives is evidence. The Spirit is given to the Christian to produce fruits of righteousness. When this fruit is manifest, this is proof that the Spirit is present and working in that life. This fruit is listed in Gal. 5:22-23: "Love, joy, peace, longsuffering, kindness, goodness, faithfulness, meekness, and self-control." Paul definitely says in Romans 5:5: "The love of God hath been shed abroad in our hearts through the Holy Spirit which was given unto us." This is the scond proof of His presence.

3.   We may know that we possess the Spirit because He testifies to the Lordship of Jesus. "No man can say, Jesus is Lord, but in the Holy Spirit" (I Cor. 12:3; cf., I Jn. 4:2). The Holy Spirit convicts the sinner of sin and leads him to confess Christ as Lord (Jn. 16:8-11; cf., Rom. 10:9-10). Then He comes to live with him and helps him to continue acknowledging Jesus as the Lord of his life. "By keeping His commandments we prove to ourselves and to others that Jesus is our Lord."[1] This proves the presence of the Spirit in one's life.

III.   BLESSINGS THE HOLY SPIRIT BRINGS

The night before Jesus' death, He was comforting and strengthening His disciples for His departure from earth to heaven. He said: "I will not leave you desolate (orphans—comfortless); I come unto you" (John 14:18). This is how He would do it. "I will pray the Father, and He shall give you another Comforter (helper, intercessor), that He may be with

---

[1]W. A. Fite, *Did You Receive the Holy Spirit When You Believed?*

87

you forever" (John 14:16). This Helper was the Holy Spirit. He was to be like Jesus and to fulfill His place of leadership with the disciples. Here are some of the blessings He brings to Christ's followers.

A. *He enables the Christian to bear fruits of righteousness.* In Galatians 5:22-23, these graces are called "the fruit of the Spirit." They are spiritual fruit that the Spirit makes to grow in one's life. Love in our hearts is the work of the Holy Spirit (Rom. 5:5). We could not develop these alone. But when we earnestly desire these graces, the Holy Spirit furnishes the power to attain them (cf. Eph. 3:14-19).

B. *He brings power to help the Christian overcome sin.* "If by the Spirit ye put to death the deeds of the body, ye shall live" (Rom. 8:13b). In the first part of this verse Paul wrote that, "If you live by the flesh, you are on the road to death" (Rom. 8:13a-Mof). The Christian is in a life and death struggle with sin. If sin wins then death is the end—"for the wages of sin is death" (Rom. 6:23). If the Christian is to live then sin must be put to death in his life. It is "Kill or be killed". In this struggle the Holy Spirit joins with the Christian to enable him to overcome. It is done by an *act* of the will, and with the *aid* of the Holy Spirit. We furnish the *purpose,* or the determination to overcome sin, and the Spirit furnishes the *power* to do it (Eph. 3:16). Victory is won through a joint effort between the Christian and the Holy Spirit. What a blessing this is! Paul exults: "For God gave us not a spirit of fearfulness; but of *power* and love and discipline" (II Tim. 1:7).

C. *The Holy Spirit seals the Christian.* ". . . in whom (Christ), having also believed, ye were sealed with the Holy Spirit of promise, (or 'as promised')" (Eph. 1:13). There were a variety of seals in ancient times. A seal was a device bearing a design, a name, or some words so made that it could impart an impression upon a soft substance like clay or wax. When the clay or wax hardened, it permanently bore the impression of the seal. A seal was used for various reasons. The two principal ones were:

1. As a mark of authenticity and authority to letters, royal commands, and similar documents (I Kings 21:8; Esther 3:12; 8:10). Today seals are used on government documents, college diplomas, etc. to show that they are true and authentic.

Paul used the word "seal" to describe his converts at Corinth. "If to others I am not an apostle, yet at least I am to you; for the seal of mine apostleship are ye in the Lord" (I Cor. 9:2). They were the proof or vindication of his apostleship. The presence of the Holy Spirit in one's life is evidence of his approval and acceptance with God. He has been authenticated by God's seal. Paul says: "And *because ye are sons,* God sent forth the Spirit of his Son into our hearts, crying, 'Abba, Father' " (Gal. 4:6).

2. As a sign of ownership. Today, even as then, men stamp their products with a seal or mark of ownership. The cattle rancher recognizes his cattle by the brand mark on them. God recognizes His own by His brand mark—the Holy Spirit. "Howbeit the firm foundation of God standeth, having this seal, The Lord knoweth them that are his" (II Tim. 2:19).

Men brand things, or seal them because they are valuable to them—they do not want to lose them or have them stolen. Believers are precious to God—they were purchased with the blood of His beloved Son. He has placed His stamp of approval and ownership in them—the Spirit. Paul writes: "But if any man hath not the Spirit of Christ, he is none of his" (Rom. 8:9).

D. *He intercedes for the Christian and provides power for prayer.* "And in like manner the Spirit also helpeth our infirmity: for we know not how to pray as we ought; but the Spirit himself maketh intercession for us with groanings which cannot be uttered; and he that searcheth the hearts knoweth what is the mind of the Spirit, because he maketh intercession for the saints according to the will of God" (Rom. 8:26-27; cf., Eph. 6:18; Jude 20).

We all want to pray effectively, but we often have trouble. We are weak in prayer. Many times we do not know what to pray for, nor how. Paul beautifully pictures the Holy Spirit taking hold at our side at the very time of our weakness and furnishing the power we need. How does He help?

Would it not be in the assistance granted to the Christian so as to enable him to intelligently form a petition to the Father through the Son? Under the duress of sorrow, or pain, or disappointment, we have nothing but inarticulate sighs and groans to offer in prayer. The

Holy Spirit does his intercessory work with these groans and sighs. He reads the deepest need of the human heart—he knows the heart of the Father. The groans and signs of the Christian are made intelligible by the Spirit—the Holy Spirit helps to make meaningful the communication to God through the Son.[1]

Roy Key in his lecture "The Spirit and the Prayer Life" writes: "God does not listen simply or even primarily to our words. He listens to *us*, to our deepest groans and sighs, to our heart hunger, to the cry of our nerve cells and bone marrow. The fact is that *we* (not our words) are our real prayer, and sometimes our deepest yearning is not at all what our words are saying."[2]

In summary, the Holy Spirit provides Power in prayer by taking our "unspeakable yearnings" and as our prayer partner interprets them correctly to God. Secondly, He "intercedes and pleads (before God) in behalf of the saints according to and in harmony with God's Will" (Rom. 8:27-AMP; cf. Psa. 139:1-2).

In Romans 8:34 Paul states that Christ also makes intercession for the saints. Christ intercedes for us from his exalted place in the presence of the Father; whereas the Spirit makes intercession from within the believer. How wonderful God is to provide such matchless assistance in prayer! Weakness in prayer must surely result from man's failure to surrender his will to that of the Father's when he prays. Our prayer should be:

Have Thine own way, Lord, Have Thine own way!
Hold o'er my being Absolute sway!
Fill with Thy Spirit Till all shall see
Christ only, always, living in me!

E. *The Spirit Sustains the Christian in Hope.* "For we through the Spirit by faith wait for the hope of righteousness" (Gal. 5:5). That hope includes the return of Christ, bodily resurrection, eternity with God. These are promised to the Christian because of the righteousness brought to him through the Gospel. The Spirit sustains us in that hope.

In another connection, the Spirit is called the "earnest of

---

[1] *De Welt, Don, The Power of the Holy Spirit,* (College Press, 1963), p. 29.
[2] *The Holy Spirit in Our Lives Today*—Edited by Carl Ketcherside, p. 48.

our inheritance" (Eph. 1:14). Paul mentions the "first fruits of the Spirit" (Rom. 8:23). The word "earnest" means "pledge", or "downpayment" of our eternal inheritance. The Spirit has been given to the Christian as a foretaste of the bliss to come. Like earnest money, it is God's pledge that He will give us all the riches which His loving heart has provided. The Spirit helps us remain faithful until this "blessed hope" becomes a reality.

F. *The presence of the Spirit assures the believer's resurrection.* "But if the Spirit of him that raised up Jesus from the dead dwelleth in you, he that raised up Christ Jesus from the dead shall give life also to your mortal bodies through his Spirit that dwelleth in you" (Rom. 8:11; cf., I Cor. 6:14). If we die in Christ, God through the Spirit will raise us from the grave to be clothed with the new body He has prepared (II Cor. 5:1-2).

What manifold blessings the Spirit brings to the believer! When man is lost in sin, the Spirit convicts him of sin and leads him to Christ and forgiveness. Then the Spirit comes to live in the Christian to be his "Paraclete" or Helper in living faithfully until death (Rev. 2:10). The believer is then assured of his ressurection and eternal life with God because the Spirit dwells in him. What more could the Spirit do to assure our salvation? Thanks to God who giveth us His Spirit!

IV. OUR OBLIGATION OR RESPONSE TO THE INDWELLING SPIRIT

With all these blessings there comes also a responsibility on the part of man. Some of these obligations are:

A. *Not to Grieve the Spirit.* "And grieve not the Holy Spirit of God, in whom ye were sealed unto the day of redemption" (Eph. 4:30). The context of this verse indicates that the Spirit is grieved by corrupt speech, lying, stealing, malice, anger, and unforgiveness. Being the temple of God on earth (I Cor. 3:16; 6:19; Eph. 2:19-22) we must conduct ourselves as worthy of this honored and heavenly Guest. We cannot afford for Him to leave us!

B. *We are not to Quench the Spirit.* "Quench not the Spirit" (I Thess. 5:19).

The word "quench" suggests a smothered fire—the

91

Holy Spirit, however, is not an inanimate object but is a person. It is easy to recall the reaction of a loved one who becomes discouraged by an opposing attitude. The fire of enthusiasm is smothered by a cold response. Just so with the Holy Spirit of God. He wants to fill our lives with all His blessed fruit; when we refuse to decide in His favor, His power and presence within us are quenched or smothered.[1]

As a fire may be smothered by too much non-combustible matter so the zeal of the Christian may be quenched and the work of the Spirit hindered by the cares of this world. A fire will also die from an absence of fuel. The Holy Spirit through His word may persuade us to do many things, but if we refuse or neglect them we have frustrated the work of the Spirit in our lives.

C. *We are to walk by the Spirit.* Rather than grieve or quench the Spirit the New Testament urges us to walk by the Spirit. "If we live by the Spirit, by the Spirit let us also walk" (Gal. 5:25).

Paul makes a distinction between *living* and *walking* by the Spirit. "It we live by the Spirit, let us also walk by the Spirit" (Gal. 5:25). Walking by the Spirit is a more advanced spiritual life than living by the Spirit; for it means not only living by the Spirit but being led, guided, energized and helped in all things said and done, day after day. Such a life becomes a real power for God in the church and community. All of one's talents and time, money and gifts, positions and skills are used for the glory of Christ, for they are all placed at His disposal and used by His Spirit. Only by a complete surrender and a full dedication may we reach that climateric experience of "walking by the Spirit."[1]

---

[1]Don DeWelt, *The Power of The Holy Spirit,* College Press, p. 32.
[1]W. A. Fite, "Did You Receive the Holy Spirit When You Believed?" (Tract)

REVIEW QUESTIONS—PERSON AND GIFT OF
THE HOLY SPIRIT

TRUE-FALSE:

1. _____ The Holy Spirit and the Word are inseparable and identical.
2. _____ The Spirit should be referred to as "it."
3. _____ The Holy Spirit helped create the world.
4. _____ One can know he has the Spirit by the emotion he feels.

COMPLETE:

1. Two evidences that one has the Spirit are:
   (1) _____
   (2) _____
2. List three blessings the Holy Spirit brings:
   (a) _____
   (b) _____
   (c) _____
3. Explain the phrase "sealed with the Holy Spirit":

   _____

   _____

   _____

IX
BAPTISM IN THE HOLY SPIRIT

I. The Promise of the Baptism in the Holy Spirit.
   A. Joel prophesied it.
   B. John the Baptist predicted it.
   C. Jesus Promised the Baptism in the Holy Spirit.

II. The Promise Fulfilled.
   A. Pentecost.
      1. Characteristics of the Baptism.
      2. Who received the Baptism in the Spirit.
      3. Why is this manifestation of the called a "Baptism"?
   B. Cornelius Baptized in the Spirit.
      1. Manner of receiving the Baptism.
      2. Evidence that this was the Baptism in the Holy Spirit.

III. The Purpose for the Baptism in the Holy Spirit.
   A. Pentecost.
   B. Purpose of the Baptism to Cornelius.

IV. Do Christians Receive the Baptism in the Holy Spirit today?
   A. Promised only to Apostles.
   B. Jesus gave no conditions for receiving the Baptism.
   C. The purposes for which it was given have been fulfilled.
   D. Paul states that there is only ONE Baptism.

V. The Need for Using Scriptural Names for Scriptural Acts.

BAPTISM IN THE HOLY SPIRIT

What is the Baptism in the Holy Spirit? Some people think that it is another name for conversion. Theodore Epp wrote:

93

"Every believer in Christ was baptized by the Holy Spirit into the Body of Christ the moment he believed."[1] John F. Walvoord says in his book, *The Holy Spirit*:

> *Salvation and baptism coextensive.* One of the prevailing misconceptions of the baptism of the Holy Spirit is the notion that it is a special ministration enjoyed by only a few Christians. On the contrary, the Scriptures make it plain that every Christian is baptized by the Holy Spirit at the moment of salvation. Salvation and baptism are therefore coextensive, and it is impossible to be saved without this work of the Holy Spirit.[2]

The proof-text most often used to support this view is I Corinthians 12:13: "For by one Spirit are we all baptized into one body." However, this can be translated: "For *by the means of* or *through the agency of* the one spirit were we all baptized into one body." The Amplified Version so translates it (See Matt. 9:34; I Cor. 14:21 for similar translations of the Greek word *En*).

The meaning is that the Holy Spirit was the agent that convicted us of sin and led us to obedience in baptism. Through that act we were brought into the body of Christ, the Church, and received the gift of the Holy Spirit as Peter promised (Acts 2:38).

The baptism in the Holy Spirit is *not* synonymous with conversion. What is it then? There are only *two* experiences in the New Testament that are designated baptism in the Spirit: Acts 2:1-4, the outpouring of the Spirit on Pentecost; and Acts 10:44-46, the second outpouring of the Spirit on the Gentiles in the house of Cornelius. Please read Acts 1:4-5, and Acts 11:15-16 for confirmation of this. When we speak of the baptism in the Holy Spirit in this chapter, we will be referring to those two events.

---

[1] Epp, Theodore, *The Other Comforter*, (The Good News Broadcasting Association, Inc., 1966), p. 72.

[2] De Welt, Don, *The Power of the Holy Spirit*, (College Press, 1963), p. 40.

I. THE PROMISE OF THE BAPTISM IN THE HOLY SPIRIT

A. *Joel prophesied it.* "And it shall come to pass afterward, that I will pour out my Spirit upon all flesh . . ." (Joel 2:28). On the day of Pentecost, Peter explained the wonderful happenings as "this is that which hath been spoken through the Prophet Joel" (Acts 2:16). This was the beginning of the Age of the Holy Spirit.

B. *John the Baptist predicted it.* "I indeed baptize you in water unto repentance; but he that cometh after me is mightier than I, . . . he shall baptize you in the Holy Spirit and in fire" (Matt. 3:11; cf. Mark 1:8; Luke 3:16). John did not say when this baptism would occur or who would receive it. He simply said that Jesus would baptize in the Holy Spirit and in fire. The word "fire" in Matthew 3:10-12 symbolizes judgment. Note that the unfruitful tree is burned with fire (v. 10), likewise the chaff (v. 12). Obviously the baptism of fire in v. 11, refers to the judgment of God on those who reject Christ and the Gospel (See II Thess. 1:7-9).

C. *Jesus Promised the Baptism in the Holy Spirit.* "And behold, I send forth the promise of my Father upon you; but tarry ye in the city, until ye be clothed with power from on high" (Luke 24:49). Jesus reminded His Apostles just before the ascension, "But ye shall receive power, when the Holy Spirit is come upon you; and ye shall be my witnesses both in Jerusalem, and all Judaea and Samaria, and unto the uttermost part of the earth" (Acts 1:8). The apostles were to wait for the "power" before they began preaching the Gospel. This they did.

II. THE PROMISE FULFILLED

Just before the ascension of Christ, Jesus told the Apostles, "Ye shall be *baptized* in the Holy Spirit *not many days hence*" (Acts 1:5). Since Jesus had been on the earth forty days after His resurrection (Acts 1:3), it was only ten days until Pentecost—the day the Holy Spirit came (Acts 2:1-4). Let us examine this first example of the baptism in the Holy Spirit.

A. *Pentecost.*

1. Characteristics of the Baptism. Jesus had told the apostles to wait in Jerusalem. They did. When the Holy Spirit

95

came it was announced and made known by three outward manifestations.

(a) Sound. "And suddenly there came from heaven a sound as of the rushing of a mighty wind, and it filled all the house where they were sitting" (Acts 2:2). The sound was not wind, but it sounded like a great wind—perhaps like the roar of a tornado. The Greek word *akos* translated "sound" is used in Luke 21:25 to describe the roar of the sea. The sound "came from heaven" and as it neared earth became louder until it reached its climax in the temple where the apostles were.

Luke says it "filled all the house where they were sitting" (Acts 2:2); like "as a bath is filled with water, that they might be baptized with the Holy Ghost, in fulfillment of Acts 1:5" (Canon Cook).[1]

The obvious purpose for the sound was to announce the coming of the Holy Spirit and to bring the people to the temple. This purpose was accomplished. "And when this sound was heard, the multitude came together . . ." (Acts 2:6). The Lord wanted a crowd when His apostles preached the first Gospel message!

(b) Light. "And there appeared to them tongues resembling fire, which were separated and distributed and that settled on each one of them" (Acts 2:3-AMP). The audible sign—the sound, was followed by a visible one—light. It was not fire, but it was a bright light that looked like fire. In the Old Testament fire had been to the Jews, a symbol of the Divine presence. For example, God appeared to Moses in the burning bush, and on Mt. Sinai in fire (Ex. 3:2; Deut. 5:4; see also the pillar of fire that led Israel-Ex. 13:21). This brilliant light would emphasize God's presence that day.

In addition to symbolizing God's presence in the Spirit, the light also pointed out the apostles and made the multitude aware of them. The Greek word for "parting asunder" means to "cleave asunder", or cut in pieces as a butcher does meat. The light apparently appeared from heaven in one shaft of light, then divided itself and pointed a fiery finger of light at the head of each apostle. With this heavenly "spotlight" shining on the

[1]Robertson, A. T., *Acts of the Apostles,* (Broadman Press, 1930), p. 21.

apostles, every one should have been aware that these men were God's men!

(c)   Languages. "And they were all filled with the Holy Spirit, and began to speak with other tongues (languages) as the Spirit gave them utterance. Now there were dwelling at Jerusalem Jews, devout men, from every nation under heaven. And when this sound was heard, the multitude came together, and were confounded, because that every man heard them speaking in his own language" (Acts 2:4-6).

The Spirit empowered the apostles to speak in languages they had never studied. This was the miracle. This confounded the Jews who were present from nations all over the Mid-East and Europe. "And they were all amazed and marvelled, saying, Behold are not all these that speak Galileans? And how hear we, *every man in our own language wherein we were born?*" (Acts 2:7-8). The apostles were speaking known languages. They were understood by those who knew the languages. The Galileans were not noted for scholarship—yet they were speaking these foreign languages. It had to be a miracle of God!

These three phenomena—sound, light, and languages were given to call the people together, center their attention on the apostles, and make them realize that this was from God. This prepared them for Peter's sermon (Acts 2:14-36).

2.   Who received the Baptism in the Spirit? Bible scholars do not agree on the answer. Some believe that the one hundred and twenty mentioned in Acts 1:15, received it. Others say only the twelve apostles. The latter answer seems to be better substantiated by Scripture. Note these facts:

(a)   Jesus promised it to the twelve (Acts 1:2-5). In verse 5, Jesus said, "Ye shall be baptized in the Holy Spirit not many days hence." Who are the "ye" Jesus was addressing? The subject of the pronoun "ye" is in verse 2—"the apostles". No mention is made of the one hundred and twenty.

(b)   The "they" in Acts 2:1 refers to the apostles. "And when the day of Pentecost was now come, *they* were all together in one place." The grammatical rule is that a pronoun refers back to the last subject mentioned unless for some reason clearly stated in the text it would go back to a previous subject. In this scripture the last subject is "the apostles" (Acts 1:26).

97

In the original Greek there were no chapter or verse divisions like we have today. It reads like this: "And the lot fell upon Matthias; and he was numbered with the eleven apostles. And when the day of Pentecost was now come, *they* were all together in one place" (Acts 1:26; 2:1). It is clearly speaking of the twelve apostles.

(c)   Only the twelve are mentioned in Acts 2:14: "But Peter standing up with the eleven, . . ." If the one hundred and twenty received the Baptism why are only the twelve mentioned here?

(d)   The convicted Jews addressed their questions to the Apostles. "Now when they heard this, they were pricked in their heart, and said unto Peter and the rest of the apostles, Brethren, what shall we do?" (Acts 2:37). Why mention only the apostles, if all one hundred and twenty were present? The evidence would indicate that only the Apostles received the baptism in the Holy Spirit on Pentecost.

3.   Why is this manifestation of the Spirit called a "Baptism"? A brief review of the apostles' actions on Pentecost will reveal why. "And they were all *filled* with the Holy Spirit, and began to speak with other tongues, as the Spirit gave them utterance" (Acts 2:4). When they were "filled" the Spirit took over their spirits, minds, and bodies.

The word baptism, literally means "immersion." They were immersed in the Spirit.

"As the body, when baptized in water, is sunk beneath its surface and completely overwhelmed, so their spirits were completely under the control of the Holy Spirit, their very words being his and not theirs.
The metaphor is justified by the absolute power which the divine Spirit exerted upon their spirits. Such is not the case with the ordinary influences of the Spirit, consequently these are not styled baptisms in the Spirit."[1]

In only two instances is the work of the Holy Spirit called a "baptism": Pentecost and the outpouring of the Spirit on Cornelius (Acts 1:5; 11:16). In both cases the Spirit overwhelmed those receiving His power. Let us examine the case of Cornelius in Acts 10 and 11.

---

[1]McGarvey, J. W., *New Commentary on Acts of Apostles*, (Standard Publishing Company), p. 23-24.

B. *Cornelius Baptized in the Spirit.* God had said through the prophet Joel, "I will pour out my Spirit upon all flesh" (Joel 2:28). This evidently meant representatives of all mankind, since He does not give His Spirit to unbelievers (John 14:17). In the days of Jesus, Jews and Gentiles constituted "all flesh". Those who were not Jews were Gentiles. Proselytes to Judaism were considered Jews.

At Pentecost the Jews received the Spirit. The Apostles were Jews. Ten years later, Cornelius, who was a Gentile received the Baptism in the Holy Spirit (Acts 10). Now "all flesh" had received the Holy Spirit.

1. Manner of receiving the Baptism. God sent an angel to this devout Roman soldier to instruct him to "send to Joppa, and fetch Simon, whose surname is Peter; who shall speak unto thee words, whereby thou shalt be saved, thou and all thy house" (Acts 11:13-14). God sent Peter a vision of the unclean animals, and then directed him by the Spirit, to "go with them, nothing doubting; for I have sent them" (Acts 10:20).

Peter went and preached to Cornelius and his friends. "While Peter yet spake these words, the Holy Spirit fell on all them that heard the word. And they of the circumcision (six Jews that Peter brought with him—Acts 11:12) that believed were amazed, . . . because that on the Gentiles also was poured out the gift of the Holy Spirit. For they heard them speak with tongues, and magnify God" (Acts 10:44-46).

2. Evidence that this was the Baptism in the Holy Spirit. We have stated that there are only two instances of baptism in the Holy Spirit—here and on Pentecost. Jesus told the Apostles "Ye shall be baptized in the Holy Spirit not many days hence" (Acts 1:5). We know that what occurred on Pentecost was a baptism in the Holy Spirit because Jesus said it was! Consider this proof that the event at Cornelius' house was also a baptism:

(a) It came directly from heaven. Luke said that it "fell on all them", and it "was poured out" on them (Acts 10:44-45; cf. Acts 2:2).

(b) It was immediately known to be the Baptism in the Holy Spirit. The Jews with Peter were amazed that the Gentiles had also received this baptism like the Jews had. The various ways by which they recognized it is not stated. The speaking in languages was a chief one (Acts 10:4b). It is doubtful that the sound and light were present since there was no need to assemble a crowd or identify Peter (Acts 10:33).

(c) It reminded Peter of the Promise of the Baptism in the Holy Spirit. "And I remembered the word of the Lord, how he said, John indeed baptized with water; but ye shall be baptized in the Holy Spirit" (Acts 11:16). If this were not a baptism, why would he be reminded of it?

(d) Peter said it was the same as Pentecost. "And as I began to speak the Holy Spirit fell on them, *even as on us at the beginning*" (Acts 11:15).

Other than the absence of the sound and light this manifestation of the Holy Spirit is the same as Pentecost (Acts 2:1-4). These are the only two that are called "baptism in the Holy Spirit." They are the only two that have the same characteristics and therefore should be called "baptisms." This should be convincing proof that what occurred in the house of Cornelius was the Baptism in the Holy Spirit.

III. THE PURPOSE FOR THE BAPTISM IN THE HOLY SPIRIT

A. *Pentecost.* Jesus gave the purpose for the Holy Spirit being given to the Apostles in Acts 1:8—"Ye shall receive *power,* when the Holy Spirit is come upon you; and *ye shall be my witnesses* both in Jerusalem, and in all Judaea and Samaria, and unto the uttermost part of the earth." Simply stated, the apostles were baptized in the Holy Spirit to empower and equip them to do the work Jesus gave them to do. That was: (1) to witness to Christ's Resurrection and the salvation in Him, and (2) to establish and lead the Lord's Church which began on Pentecost. Here are some of the specific reasons:

1. To give them power for teaching. Jesus told the apostles in the upper room that when the Holy Spirit came "he shall teach you all things, and bring to your remembrance all that I said unto you" (John 14:26). The apostles were the divinely inspired teachers of the church (See Acts 2:42; 6:2-4). The Holy Spirit empowered them. He did it in two ways: First, He enabled them to recall the teachings Jesus had given them;

100

and secondly, He revealed new truths which Jesus had not had time to teach them (See John 16:12-13). This is why the church "Continued steadfastly in the apostles' teaching . . ." (Acts 2:42). In addition to their personal teaching, they were empowered to write the New Testament for our instruction today.

2. Power to perform miracles to confirm the Word. In Mark 16:17 several miracles are listed which the apostles and early Christians would do. In verse 20 the purpose for the miracles is given. "And they went forth, and preached everywhere, the Lord working with them, *and confirming the word by the signs that followed.*" The miracles performed by the Power of the Spirit proved these men to be God's messengers.

3. Power to impart spiritual gifts to others. In addition to the miraculous powers the apostles personally possessed, they were able to impart special powers to others. Peter and John laid their hands on the Samaritan Christians and they received special powers (Acts 8:14-19). Paul did the same to the men at Ephesus and they received the gifts of tongues and prophecy (Acts 19:1-7). There is no clear evidence of anyone except the apostles having such powers. It would seem to be part of the "power" given them through the Baptism in the Holy Spirit.

4. Power to establish, lead, and discipline the church. In summary, the Holy Spirit gave the apostles whatever power they needed to establish the church on Pentecost and lead it through its formative years. The apostles guided the infant church in worship (Acts 2:42; 20:7); and in church organization—selection of deacons, then elders (Acts 6:1-7; 14:23; 11:30). Through them God administered corrective discipline—like the death of Ananias and Sapphira (Acts 5:1-11). The apostles maintained a certain supervision over the expanding church. Peter and John were sent to Samaria, and Barnabas was sent to Antioch. They were to approve the developments and lend a helping hand (Acts 8:14-17; 11:1-26).

The Holy Spirit was a true Helper to the Apostles by furnishing the wisdom and power to do their work of Kingdom building.

B. *Purpose of the Baptism to Cornelius.* The case of Cornelius is unique. It is the only instance in the New Testament of the Holy Spirit being given to a non-Christian. There must have been a special reason for this exception. There was! In order to understand it, the relation of Jews to Gentiles must be understood. For ten years the church was composed of Jews or proselytes only. When the church began the apostles and evangelists preached only to Jews; race wise it was a Jewish church. Christ had died for *all* but *all* were not hearing the good newsof His atoning death.

The Jews' prejudice against the Gentiles constituted a serious race problem. A Jew would not enter a Gentile's home, nor let one enter his. If he touched a Gentile in the market place he took a bath when he reached home. He did not speak to one unless absolutely necessary. To sit down and eat with a Gentile was unthinkable to a devout Jew.

To correct this sad situation God did four things to bring about the conversion of the Gentiles. First He sent an angel to tell Cornelius to send for the apostle Peter. He gave a vision to Peter to teach him not to consider any man "common or unclean." The Holy Spirit then commanded Peter to go with the men from Cornelius. For the final convincing act God baptized Cornelius and his Gentile friends in the Holy Spirit (Acts 10:1-48).

It may be asked, "but why the overwhelming gift of the Baptism?" The answer is that anything less would not have convinced the Jews to fully accept the Gentiles as Christians. They would have looked upon the Gentiles as "second rate" Christians. (Some did anyway—See Acts 15). Peter made clear the equality of the Gentiles at the Conference on Circumcision when he said: "And God, who knoweth the heart, bare them (Gentiles) witness, giving them the Holy Spirit, *even as he did unto us*; and *he made no distinction between us and them*" (Acts 15:8-9).

This fact is further confirmed by the reaction of the church in Jerusalem when Peter defended himself for preaching to Cornelius. In his defense (Acts 11:1-18) Peter relates the four things God did to convince him and concludes, "If then God gave unto them the *like gift* as he did also unto us, . . . who was I, that I could withstand God?" (Acts 11:17). Peter concluded that God's will was so clear in this matter, that he would have been resisting God, not to have baptized Cornelius into Christ. The other leaders upon hearing this, "held their peace, and glorified God, saying, Then to the Gentiles *also* hath God granted repentance unto life" (Acts 11:18). The purpose for the Baptism in the Holy Spirit to Cornelius was *to convince the Jews that the Gentiles were to hear the Gospel and be saved also.*

IV. DO CHRISTIANS RECEIVE THE BAPTISM IN THE HOLY SPIRIT TODAY?

The answer would be No, the New Testament does not promise the Baptism in the Spirit to Christians today. Here are the facts regarding this:

A. *When Christ was on earth he did not promise the Baptism in the Holy Spirit to all Christians—only to the Apostles.* In Acts 1:5 Jesus said "but ye shall be baptized in the Holy Spirit not many days hence." The "ye" refers to the apostles in verse 2. There is no indication that he was talking to anyone else when he made this promise. Cornelius was baptized in the Holy Spirit but had not been promised the gift he received. Jesus is the administrator of baptism in the Holy Spirit. He alone decides who receives it. If he so wishes he can baptize anyone in the Holy Spirit in any age. But, in the New Testament he did not promise it to anyone except the apostles.

B. *Jesus gave no conditions for receiving the Baptism.* In order to receive the Holy Spirit as an indwelling Presence, Peter said there were conditions to be met. He said to the people who believed in Jesus to "Repent" and "be baptized for the remission of sins" in order to receive the gift of the Spirit (Acts 2:38).

But no such instructions were given for the Baptism in the Holy Spirit. The only instruction given the apostles was "tarry ye in the city, (Jerusalem) until ye be clothed with power from on high" (Luke 24:49). Merrill Unger referring to those who received the Spirit on Pentecost wrote:

> Nothing they did or said could in one iota affect the matter of the coming of the Spirit. They were not told to pray, but merely to 'sit' to 'wait' (Luke 24:29), which only meant that they were not to attempt any work of 'witnessing' (Acts 1:8) until the Holy Spirit came to enable them. Of course, they prayed (1:14), and had won-

derful fellowship, but all this was unconnected with the coming of the Spirit, who came by the divine 'promise' (Luke 24:49), at a divinely scheduled time (Acts 2:1), at a divinely designated place (Joel 2:32), in accordance with Old Testament type (Lev. 23:15-22). Had they been tarrying in any other place except Jerusalem, where they were told to wait, they would not have received the promise. 'For in Mount Zion, and in Jerusalem, shall be deliverance, as the Lord hath said' (Joel 2:32).[1]

C. *The purposes for which the Baptism was given have been fulfilled.* The purposes can be summarized under three heading: (1) To empower the apostles for the special work they had been called to do for Christ; (2) To provide divine credentials for them as God's spokesmen; (3) To convince the Jews that the Gentiles were also included in the Scheme of Redemption. These purposes have been fulfilled, therefore, we conclude that the special measure of the Spirit called the Baptism is not needed or extended to Christians today.

D. *Paul states that there is only ONE Baptism.* Ephesians 4:5 states "one Lord, one faith, one baptism, one God and Father of all . . ." Paul wrote the Letter to Ephesus about 62-63 A. D. At that time there was one baptism in the church. What was it? Five baptisms are mentioned in the New Testament. They are: (1) John's Baptism—a literal act performed by John preparing the way for Jesus (Luke 7:29-30). (2) Baptism of suffering—used figuratively—of Jesus' suffering and death (Mark 10:38-39). (3) Baptism of fire—figuratively—referring to the punishment of the wicked (Matt. 3:11-12). (4) Baptism in the Holy Spirit (Acts 1:4-5). (5) Great Commission or Christian Baptism—a literal immersion in water of a penitent believer in Christ (Matt. 28:19-20; Acts 2:38).

Which one of these would be so vital and permanent as to be called by Paul the "one baptism"? John's baptism fulfilled its purpose when Jesus came, and was replaced by His new command (Matt. 28:19-20). Describing suffering as a baptism would hardly place it in this highly important position. The baptism of fire is for the wicked, and would not be listed in this seven-fold

[1]Unger, Merrill F., *The Baptizing Work of the Holy Spirit,* (Dhnham Publishing Company), p. 57.

summary of the Christian Faith. This leaves Holy Spirit and Christian baptism. Any serious student of the Word knows that Christian or believer's baptism is a permanent ordinance in the church. That being true, then baptism in the Holy Spirit obviously fulfilled it's purpose on Pentecost and in the house of Cornelius and was nullified. This leaves Jesus' Great Commission baptism as the "one baptism" Paul had in mind.

V. THE NEED FOR USING SCRIPTURAL NAMES FOR SCRIPTURAL ACTS

For emphasis, let it be stated that in no way is it the purpose of this study to minimize or degrade the work of the Holy Spirit in the church today. The purpose of these lessons is to emphasize the vital place of the Holy Spirit in the church in all ages. This is especially needed in the church now. Our aim has been to call men's attention to this Great Comforter and Helper who is still leading and empowering God's workers to the glory of Christ and the saving of souls. We do desire however to rightly divide the Word so that we will not attribute things to the Holy Spirit that the Word does not. We desire every gift and power which God wants us to have. But we shrink from deceiving ourselves or other people by teaching them to expect things that God has not promised.

Many people are claiming great experiences from God today, and calling them the Baptism in the Holy Spirit.

"But calling such experiences the Baptism in the Holy Spirit does not mean that what occurred was the Baptism in the Holy Spirit! Unless the Word of God identifies an experience by designating it, we have no right to identify it and designate it with only human authority! Something wonderful and glorious may have happened to some folk of our day, but please, please, *call Bible things by Bible names!*"[1]

---

[1] De Welt, Don. *The Power of the Holy Spirit.* (College Press, 1963), p. 43.

REVIEW QUESTIONS—BAPTISM IN THE HOLY SPIRIT

FILL IN THE BLANKS:

1. The work of the Spirit is seen in what three areas?

   a. _____

   b. _____

   c. _____

2. What was the Baptism in the Holy Spirit and when did it occur?

   _____

   _____

   _____

3. Who received the Baptism in the Holy Spirit on Pentecost? Give Proof.

   _____

   _____

   _____

4. List the Purposes for the Baptism on Pentecost.

   a. _____

   b. _____

5. Why did Cornelius receive the Baptism in the Holy Spirit?

   _____

   _____

6. Give three reasons for *not* expecting the Baptism in the Holy Spirit today.

   a. _____

   b. _____

   c. _____

X
SPIRITUAL GIFTS

I. **What Were Spiritual Gifts?**
   A. **Explanation of these gifts.**

II. **The Manner of Giving These Gifts.**
   A. **Through Prayer and the laying on of the Apostles' hands.**
   B. **The Gift of Tongues also accompanied the baptism in the Spirit.**

III. **To Whom Given?**

IV. **Purpose for Spiritual Gifts.**
   A. **To build up the church.**
   B. **Guidance and protection of the church.**
   C. **Confirmation of the word.**

V. **Duration of the Gifts.**
   A. **They belonged to the childhood of the church.**
   B. **The means for imparting these gifts is not present today.**
   C. **Spiritual gifts are not needed today.**

SPIRITUAL GIFTS

No discussion of the Holy Spirit would be complete without a study of the gifts of the Spirit. "It should be remembered that there is a clear and definite distinction to be made between the Holy Spirit as a gift and the gifts of the Holy Spirit."[1] Acts 2:38 is an example of the former. Peter promised the believers at Pentecost that if they would repent and be immersed they would receive "the remission of sins", and "the gift of the Holy Spirit", or the Holy Spirit as a gift. Spiritual gifts on the other hand were spe-

---

[1] Boles, H. Leo, *The Holy Spirit: His Personality, Nature, Works,* (Gospel Advocate Company, 1942), p. 171.

cial powers or abilities given by the Spirit to believers to be used in the service and growth of the church.

"Such powers or abilities were called *Spiritual* because they were prompted by or through the Holy Spirit. They are referred to as *gifts* because they are gratis or not earned. They were not merited by the possessors, but were given by God out of free grace."[1]

These are part of the extraordinary powers given to the early church by the Spirit. The baptism in the Holy Spirit (Acts 2:1-4; 10:44-48); and the miraculous "fillings" of the Holy Spirit (Acts 4:8, 31; 7:55) are other examples of these extraordinary powers.

I. WHAT WERE SPIRITUAL GIFTS?

The most complete list of spiritual gifts is found in I Corinthians 12:8-11.

Here the apostle names *nine* distinct gifts which he classifies under three heads. The *first class* includes those gifts which refer to the *intellectual powers* —"the word of wisdom," "the word of knowledge," and "faith." (I Cor. 12:8,9). The *second class* are the gifts which exhibit the faith of the one that possesses them—"gifts of healings," "workings of miracles," "prophecy," and "discernings of spirits." (I Cor. 12:9,10). The *third class* are the gifts of tongues—"divers kinds of tongues" and "interpretation of tongues." (I Cor. 12:10)[2]

A. *Explanation of these gifts.* It is not easy to clearly identify all these gifts since the New Testament does not explain them fully. But the following are generally accepted explanations of them.

---

[1]De Welt, Don, *The Power of the Holy Spirit,* (College Press, 1969), p. 57-58.
[2]Boles, H. Leo, *The Holy Spirit: His Personality, Nature, Works,* (Gospel Advocate Company, 1942), p. 174.

1. "Word of Wisdom." This does not refer to wisdom that comes from personal thinking, but to that wisdom which comes directly from God, or it may have been special wisdom given for specific situations (cf. James 1:5). Perhaps in each congregation one or two men were given this gift of wisdom to guide the church in making difficult decisions. Jesus had promised his followers: "I will give you a mouth and wisdom, which none of your adversaries will be able to withstand or contradict" (Luke 21:15). For illustrations see Acts 4:8-14; 6:10.

2. "Word of Knowledge." Not just ordinary knowledge that can be gained by study, but special knowledge, insight, or illumination given by the Spirit. The knowledge that enabled the possessor of the gift to take the Gospel and make practical application of it to the lives of the Christians.

3. "Faith." Not saving faith, because that comes by hearing the Word of God (Rom. 10:17). Nor is it to be confused with faith or faithfulness as a fruit of the Spirit which every Christian should possess (Gal. 5:22). But it is the faith that moves mountains—a miraculous faith (Matt. 17:20; 1 Cor. 13:2). It must be remembered that this gift of faith was given by God, and could not be demanded or expected.

4. "Gifts of healings." The gifts of healing were primarily concerned with healing of physical illness. It is listed "gifts" plural, presumably because they were empowered to heal many diseases (examples: Acts 3:1-10; 9:32-35; 28:7-10).

5. "Workings of miracles." This gift may have included healing but covered also a wider range of mighty deeds of every kind. The book of Acts lists several examples of these miracles: (a) Exorcism—the demon possessed maid at Philippi (Acts 16:16-18). (b) Resurrection—Dorcas (Acts 9:36-42). (c) Elymas struck blind (Acts 13:6-12). (d) Acts 19:11 states that Paul performed "special miracles" or "miracles of an unusual kind." The exact nature of these miracles is not indicated, but the miracle of the aprons was one example (Acts 19:12).

6. "Prophecy." Prophecy had a two-fold purpose. First it had a predictive element in it—foretelling. This is the meaning most people associate with the word. Secondly, it involved preaching—presenting God's message to man under the guidance of the Holy Spirit—forthtelling. The prophets, both Old

Testament and New Testament, did far more of the latter than the former. This gift was possessed by Agabus (Acts 11:28; 21:10); Philip's daughters (Acts 21:9); and Judas and Silas (Acts 15:32). Paul considered this gift one of the greatest because it taught and edified people (I Cor. 14:5, 18-19, 23-25).

7. "Discerning (or distinguishing) of spirits." This gift enabled the person to distinguish between true and false teachers. The apostle John admonished the church to "Believe not every spirit, but prove (test) the spirits, whether they are of God; because many false prophets are gone out into the world" (I John 4:1). John is writing of true and false teachers or prophets. Evidently a man with this gift could distinguish between them and save the church. This was very essential in the days before the New Testament was written, and when the preachers came with an oral message.

8. "Gift of tongues—languages." This gift provided the ability to speak a language which was new to and unstudied by the speaker. At Pentecost the apostles spoke in known languages "as the Spirit gave them utterance" (Acts 2:4). Luke writes that the people marvelled and asked, "Behold, are not all these that speak Galileans? And how hear we, every man *in our own language wherein we were born?"* (Acts 2:7-8).

The gift of tongues accompanied the baptism in the Holy Spirit and was a proof of it. This is seen both at Pentecost and at the house of Cornelius (Acts 10:44-46). This gift also came through the laying on of the Apostles' hands (Acts 19:1-6). A more thorough study of this subject can be found in Chapter 11.

9. "Interpretation of Tongues." This gift gave the ability to translate the languages spoken by those having the gift of tongues.

II. THE MANNER OF GIVING THESE GIFTS

A. *Through prayer and the laying on of the Apostles' hands.* There are two examples in Acts where spiritual gifts were imparted. The first is in Acts 8:14-17. Philip had been leading a great evangelistic crusade in Samaria and many had turned to the Lord. Peter and John came down from Jerusalem to help. Their primary help was the giving of spiritual gifts. Luke writes of Peter and John: "When they were come down, prayed for them, that they might receive the Holy Spirit. . . Then laid they their hands on them, and they received the Holy Spirit" (Acts 8:15, 17). Since the Samaritans had already received the Holy Spirit as a gift when they believed and were baptized (Acts 2:38), what the apostles gave were these special gifts or powers of the Spirit. These special powers were given through the apostles when they laid their hands on the Christians. Luke does not say what specific gifts were given. They must have been very appealing for Simon wanted to purchase this wonderful power for himself (Acts 8:18-19).

The second example of spiritual gifts is in Acts 19:1-6. Here the apostle Paul came to Ephesus and found disciples of John the Baptist. He thought they were disciples of Christ and asked them if they had received the Holy Spirit when they believed. He apparently was asking about these special powers. They answered: "Nay, we did not so much as hear whether the Holy Spirit was given" (Acts 19:2). Paul then learned that they were disciples of John. After teaching them, he baptized them into Christ. "And when Paul had laid his hands on them, the Holy Spirit came on them; and they spake with tongues, and prophesied" (Acts 19:6).

These are the only examples that indicate the way these powers were given. In both cases the Spirit gave them through the Apostles. Some men cite the case of Timothy as proof that other men could impart these gifts. Paul admonished Timothy, "Neglect not the gift that is in thee, which was given thee by prophecy, with the laying on of the hands of the presbytery (elders)" (II Tim. 1:6). It is not clear what gift Paul had in mind. He may have been referring to Timothy's ordination by the elders to be an evangelist. He could be urging him to use his gift of preaching. The expression "which was given thee by prophecy", makes it difficult to know exactly what is meant by this gift. This scripture does not furnish definite proof that men other than the Apostles could impart spiritual gifts.

The case of Philip in Samaria would strongly suggest that only the apostles could impart these gifts. Philip had been preaching and baptizing multitudes, but had given no gifts (Acts 8:4-13). It seems that Peter and John came from Jerusalem for the purpose of giving these gifts. Why did Philip not give them if he had the power? Philip had miraculous powers himself, (Acts 8:6-7), but he seemingly was not able to pass them on to others.

We reiterate, the only *clear* examples of the giving of these spiritual gifts was through the laying on of the *Apostles'* hands.

B. *The Gift of Tongues also accompanied the baptism in the Spirit.* The only exception to this is the gift of tongues. At Pentecost and at the house of Cornelius, the gift of tongues accompanied the baptism in the Holy Spirit (Acts 2:4; 10:46). In all other cases the spiritual gifts were given through the apostles.

III. TO WHOM GIVEN?

The people receiving the spiritual gifts were Christians. The Samaritans had been baptized by Philip (Acts 8:12). Paul had baptized the twelve men at Ephesus before the gifts were given (Acts 19:1-7). This is in harmony with Jesus statement concerning the Spirit: "whom the world cannot receive" (John 14:17).

It should be emphasized that the Holy Spirit exercised his sovereign authority in the distribution of these gifts. There is no evidence that every Christian received a gift. But rather it would indicate that they did not. Paul asked: "Have all gifts of healing? Do all speak with tongues? Do all interpretet?" (I Cor. 12:30). The implied answer is, *No.* The Spirit in His own wisdom chose the ones to receive them. Paul writes: "For to *one* is given through the Spirit the word of wisdom; and to *another* the word of knowledge . . . dividing to each one severally (or individually) *even as he wills*" (I Cor. 12:8, 11). No one was promised them, and no directions were given as to how they were to seek them. Paul told the Corinthians: "Follow after love; yet desire earnestly spiritual gifts" (I Cor. 14:1). But no specifics were given for them to do to receive them. Which obviously means they were not to seek them. If the Spirit willed to give a person a gift—he would receive it. If He did not then no gift was given.

IV. PURPOSE FOR SPIRITUAL GIFTS

A. *To build up (edify) the church.* Paul concisely gives the purpose for spiritual gifts in I Corinthians 12:7: "To each one

111

is given the manifestation of the Spirit *for the common good.*"
Those possessing gifts were to use them, "that the church may
receive edifying" (I Cor. 14:5b). Paul emphasizes, "let all things
be done unto edifying" (I Cor. 14:26b). The Greek word for
edification—*oikosomeo* is derived from *oikos* (house) and *someo*
(to build) and means literally "the building of a house". Spiritually speaking it means to strengthen, benefit, establish, or build
up (I Cor. 8:1: "Love edifieth—builds up").

"It was possible for those who possessed these extraordinary gifts to neglect them or to abuse the proper use of them . . .
All of these gifts were to be used for the general edification, and
not for self-glorification of the one who possessed the gift."[1]

How did these gifts build up or edify the church? Paul ex-
plains: "When you come together, each one has a hymn, a lesson, a revelation, a tongue, or an interpretation. Let all things
be done for edification" (I Cor. 14:26). Through singing, teaching, and relating the truths God had revealed, to them, the possessors of these gifts were building up the church. This was especially necessary since the New Testament had not been fully
written yet.

The spiritual gifts of wisdom, knowledge, and especially
prophecy were used to edify the church. Paul commends the
latter gift very highly for edification (I Cor. 14:3-5).

B. *Guidance and protection of the church.* God gave these
gifts to benefit the church. Here are some of the ways they did:

1. The gift of prophecy. An incident in Acts reveals how
the gift of prophecy was a real help to the welfare of the church.
Agabus, the prophet, went from Jerusalem down to Antioch
(Syria). He told that the Spirit had revealed to him that a great
famine would come. Immediately the brethren at Antioch sent
relief to the brethren in Judea by Barnabas and Saul. Thus the
Spirit provided for the poor saints in Jerusalem and Judea. This
shows that these gifts were used in a very practical way for the
benefit of the church.

2. The gift of discerning of spirits. This ability was given
to protect the church against false prophets who would disturb

---

[1]Boles, H. Leo, *The Holy Spirit: His Personality, Nature, Works,* (Gospel Advocate
Company, 1942), p. 174.

and destroy it by false teaching (I John 4:1). This was especially helpful in the days before the New Testament was written.

C. *Confirmation of the word.* Mark writes of the early Christians that "they went forth, and preached everywhere, the Lord working with them, and *confirming the word* by the signs (miracles) that followed" (Mark 16:20). The writer of Hebrews referring to the great salvation through the Gospel, writes: "which having at the first been spoken through the Lord, was confirmed unto us by them that heard; God also *bearing witness* with them, both by signs and wonders, and by manifold powers, and by *gifts of the Holy Spirit,* according to his own will" (Heb. 2:3-4).

The Apostles preached the Gospel and God authenticated their preaching by miracles and spiritual gifts. Paul writes: "For I will not venture to speak of anything except what Christ has wrought through me to win obedience from the Gentiles, by word and deed, by the power of signs and wonders, by the power of the Holy Spirit, so that from Jerusalem and as far round as Illyricum I have fully preached the Gospel of Christ" (Rom. 15:18-19).

Before the New Testament was written the Gospel was delivered orally. When an apostle appeared in a city and began preaching this new message he needed special powers to convince the people that what he preached was from God. There was a united effort in preaching the Gospel: the evangelists preached it—the Lord confirmed it.

V. DURATION OF THE GIFTS

That spiritual gifts were not to be permanent is clearly stated in I Corinthians 13:8-10. Prophecies were to "pass away"; tongues "will cease", and knowledge "pass away". The big question is "When?" Paul says that it will happen when "that which is perfect is come." When is that? The Greek word *Teleios* translated perfect, means: "completed, full-grown, fully."

There are two views as to when these spiritual gifts will cease: (1) They will cease when life on earth is ended and the redeemed of the Lord reach heaven—that state of absolute perfection. Then all imperfection will cease. Those who hold this view believe that spiritual gifts are still present in the church (or can be) and will be until Christ returns. (2) Others believe that the gifts ceased when the New Testament was completely written—the maturity or perfection of God's revelation, and when the last man had died who had received a spiritual gift from an Apostle.

Here are three reasons for believing that spiritual gifts ceased in the first or second century A.D.:

A. *They belonged to the "childhood" of the church.* In I Corinthians 13:11, Paul compared these gifts to his childhood speech, feelings, and thought. He continues, "Now that I am become a man, I have put away childish things." Paul implies that thes gifts are elementary helps which God had given for the establishment of the church, or for its childhood. These gifts were like scaffolding used for building a house. Once the house is completed, there is no further need for the scaffolding. Paul pleads for them to seek the permanent gifts of Faith, Hope, and Love (I Cor. 12:31; 14:la).

Prophecies, tongues and knowledge—three supernatural gifts though they were—were mortals compared with the divine spirit of love. They were needful in developing the infant church, but as that institution passed onward toward maturity and perfection (Heb. 5:12-14; 6:1; Eph. 3:14-21; 4:11-16), they were outgrown and discontinued, because from them had been developed the clear, steady light of the recorded Word, and the mature thoughtfulness and assurance of a well-instructed church. They were thrown aside, therefore, as the wheat stalk which has matured its grain; or, to use Paul's own figure, put away as the speech, feeling and judgment of childhood when they had produced their corresponding faculties in manhood. All Christians who mistakenly yearn for a renewal of these spiritual gifts, should note the clear import of these words of the apostle, which show that their presence in the church would be an evidence of immaturity and

114

weakness, rather than of fully developed power and seasoned strength.[1]

B. *The means for imparting these gifts is not present today.* These gifts were given through the laying on of the apostles' hands (Acts 8:14-17; 19:1-7). Since there are no apostles today, there is lacking the means whereby they can be given. The one exception is the gift of tongues, which accompanied the baptism in the Holy Spirit (Acts 2:1-4; 10:44-48). Since the evidence indicates that the baptism in the Holy Spirit is not given today, there is still no Scriptural means present for imparting the spiritual gifts (See chapter—Baptism in the Holy Spirit). The individual who claims to receive a spiritual gift today must explain how he received it in a way different from that revealed in the New Testament.

C. *Spiritual gifts are not needed today.*

1. Those possessing these gifts were given revelations from God for the edification of the church. Since we have the New Testament which contains the full revelation of the Gospel and God's will for man, we no longer need these special revelations.

2. They were to prove the Gospel a divine revelation, a thing unnecessary to repeat. God confirmed His preachers and their message in the first century by miracles and spiritual gifts. Once a fact has been confirmed it is unnecessary to confirm it again. With the New Testament in our hands, having been fully confirmed by God, we have all we need to bring men to Christ and establish them in him.

"We have a perfect record of these gifts which were bestowed to help confirm the preaching of the word; there was no need for a continuation of them after the full gospel had been *revealed* and *confirmed* and a *record made to preserve it.*"[2]

In summary we would say regarding spiritual gifts: "They were bestowed by the apostles only, therefore they ceased with those upon whom they had been conferred by the Holy Spirit through the apostles."[3]

[1]McGarvey, J. W., *Thessalonia,s Corinthians, Galatians and Romans,* (Standard Publishing Company, 1916), p. 131-2.

[2]Boles, H. Leo, *The Holy Spirit: His Personality, Nature, Works,* (Gospel Advocate Company, 1942), p. 175.

[3]Hoven, Victor E., *Outlines of Biblical Doctrine,* (Northwest Christian College Press, 1948), p. 87.

REVIEW QUESTIONS—SPIRITUAL GIFTS

1. Distinguish between spiritual gifts and the gift of the Holy Spirit.

   _____

   _____

2. Explain three purposes for the spiritual gifts.

   a. _____

   _____

   b. _____

   _____

   c. _____

   _____

3. How were the spiritual gifts given? _____

   _____

4. Explain two reasons why Christians should not expect these gifts today.

   a. _____

   _____

   b. _____

   _____

XI
THE GIFT OF TONGUES

I. The Gift of Tongues in the New Testament.
   A. Tongue speaking in Acts.
      1. The Apostles on Pentecost.
      2. Cornelius.
      3. The twelve disciples at Ephesus.
   B. Tongue speaking in the Corinthian church.
      1. Supposed evidence for ecstatic utterances.
      2. Evidence for human language.

II. The Purpose For the Gift of Tongues.
   A. Confirmation of the Word.
   B. Edification.
   C. A sign of the Baptism in the Holy Spirit.
   D. A sign to Israel concerning the Messiah and His Gospel.

III. Should Christians Expect the Gift of Tongues Today?
   A. The need for the gift ceased.
   B. The means of imparting these gifts are not present today.
   C. The gift of tongues was needed in the infancy of the church.
   D. The gift of tongues has not been promised to us today.

THE GIFT OF TONGUES

One might ask why a lesson on speaking in tongues or Glossolalia as it is called (from the Greek *glossa* meaning "tongue" and *laleo* meaning "to speak")? There are two reasons: First, the gift of tongues is a spiritual gift given to the early Christians by the Holy Spirit. Being a Bible doctrine, it deserves investigation.

Secondly, because of its widespread prominence in the

117

church today, it needs to be studied and understood by all Christians.

Speaking in tongues is a New Testament phenomena. There is no mention of it in the Old Testament. Jesus did not speak in tongues nor was it done while He was here on earth. Pentecost (Acts 2) is the first instance of speaking in tongues.

It is a relatively minor practice in the New Testament times. Only three books in the New Testament mention it. The Gospel of Mark has one reference to it (Mark 16:17); there are three instances of tongue speaking in the book of Acts (Acts 2:1-4; 10:44-46; 19:1-6); and only one epistle mentions it (I Cor. 12-14).

Today tongue speaking has become widespread not only among the Pentecostals but throughout Protestantism and even The Roman Catholic church. *Time* magazine called it the "fastest growing church in the hemisphere." *Life* regarded it as "the third force" (in Christianity today), equal in significance to Roman Catholicism and historic Protestantism.[1] These observations may be exaggerated but there is no major denomination today that is not affected by this movement.

Men ask, "Is this of God, or the work of man, or of Satan?" The aim of this chapter is to help answer this question.

I. THE GIFT OF TONGUES IN THE NEW TESTAMENT

A. *Tongues speaking in Acts.* The three cases of speaking in tongues in Acts are: (1) the Apostles on Pentecost (Acts 2:1-4); (2) Cornelius and his household at Caesarea (Acts 10:44-46); and (3) the twelve men at Ephesus (Acts 19:1-6). Let us examine these examples.

1. The Apostles on Pentecost. Before the Lord returned to Heaven, He instructed the Apostles to "tarry ye in the city (Jerusalem), until ye be clothed with power from on high" (Luke 24:49). For ten days they waited. On the morning of the Feast of Pentecost between eight and nine o'clock they suddenly heard a tremendous sound coming from Heaven. It came until it filled all the house where they were sitting. The sound was accompa-

---

[1]Quoted in *The Modern Tongues Movement*, Robert G. Gromacki, (The Presbyterian and Reformed Publishing Company, 1967), p. 2.

nied by a great beam of light that divided itself into fiery fingers of light which rested on the heads of the Apostles.

These signs heralded the coming of the Baptism in the Holy Spirit. The Spirit literally took over the Apostles' minds and bodies and empowered them to speak in languages they had never studied.

There were Jews attending the Feast of Pentecost from fifteen nations (Acts 2:9-11). This sound brought them rushing to the Temple where they heard the Apostles magnifying God in these foreign languages. The people were dumbfounded to hear these Galileans speaking in their native dialects (Acts 2:6). Luke writes: "And they were all amazed and marvelled, saying, Behold, are not all these that speak Galileans? And how hear we, every man in *our own language wherein we were born?*" (Acts 2:7-8).

Actual languages were spoken at Pentecost. The evidence for this is:

(a)   Some fifteen nations are listed as being present at Pentecost. Why would Luke include such a long list of countries? He wanted to make clear that the Apostles spoke in foreign languages and dialects and not in unknown sounds.

(b)   The people who knew the languages understood the Apostles. The multitude was "confounded", "amazed", "marvelled", and "perplexed." Why such a reaction? Luke answers this question when he quotes the statement of the people: "behold, are not all these that speak Galileans? and how hear we, every man *in our own language* (dialect) wherein we were born?" (Acts 2:7-8). The Apostles spoke in languages which these people understood. It also implies that they spoke with a Galilean accent. This is how they recognized them as Galileans (Acts 2:7; cf. Matt. 26:73: Mark 14:70).

The Galileans, particularly the fishermen, were not scholars or world travelers. The people knew they were seeing and hearing a miracle. They knew the Apostles could not speak in these different languages without God's help.

(c)   Luke used the words *glossa* ("tongues or languages"—Acts 2:4, 11) and *dialektos* ("dialect"—Acts 2:6, 8) interchangeably. The word dialect refers to the local form of a language. The Apostles not only spoke principal languages but

119

dialets of those languages. Pentecost was the first occurrence of speaking in tongues or languages and should thus be used to define the gift in other passages. Luke was writing to Theophilus that he might know the certainty concerning Christ and the Gospel. Therefore, Luke takes considerable pains to show Theophilus that the Apostles were speaking in distinct languages. All other examples of tongue speaking should be viewed in the light of Pentecost since this is the clearest description of what occurred.

2. Cornelius. The second instance of speaking in tongues took place in Caesarea at the house of Cornelius, the pious Gentile (Acts 10:44-48). When "the Holy Spirit fell on all them," they began to speak with tongues and magnify God. That this speaking was foreign languages is apparent for these reasons:

(a) Luke uses the same Greek word *glossa* to describe this occurrence as he did at Pentecost (Acts 10:46; cf. Acts 2:4, 11). It meant human language there, it should mean the same here, unless Luke indicated otherwise.

(b) Also, how did the Jews who accompanied Peter know that the Gentiles were magnifying God unless they could understand them? There is no mention of anyone translating. They were obviously speaking an understandable human language.

(c) In Peter's report to the Jerusalem church he said that the Gentiles had received "the like gift" (Acts 11:17) and that "the Holy Spirit fell on them, even as on us at the beginning" (Acts 11:15). This refers to Pentecost. These two statements obviously mean that the Baptism in the Spirit was the same at the house of Cornelius as at Pentecost. The speaking in tongues then should have been the same. There is no evidence to the contrary.

3. The twelve disciples at Ephesus. The third and final instance of tongue speaking in Acts is the twelve disciples of John the Baptist at Ephesus (Acts 19:1-7). Paul preached to them Jesus and baptized them into Christ. Then he laid his hands on them: "and they spake with tongues, and prophesied" (Acts 19:6). Luke again used the Greek word *glossa* as he did in the other two accounts. There is no logical reason to assume that the languages here were any different from Pentecost and Cornelius.

B. *Tongue speaking in the Corinthian church.* The only

120

mentionof the gift of tongues in the Epistles is in I Corinthians 12-14. There is little debate over the conclusion that in Acts the tongues were intelligent languages. In Corinth, though, many believe that the tongue speaking was different. Some statements by Paul lead some scholars to think he is talking about ecstatic utterances rather than human languages. This is the position of most Pentecostal and tongue speakers today.

1. Supposed evidence for ecstatic utterances. Some of the arguments in favor of interpreting *glossa* in I Corinthians 14 as unknown sounds or "the language of ecstasy" (I Cor. 14:2-NEB) are thought to be found in the text itself. The arguments are as follows:

(1) The speech is addressed to God (verses 2, 28).

(2) The speaker in the spirit speaks mysteries (verse 2).

(3) The speaker edifies himself and not others (verse 4).

(4) The speaker's understanding is unfruitful (verse 14).

(5) The speech was not understood by the hearers (verse 16).

(6) Outsiders hearing the speech will think it is madness (verse 23).[1]

It is true that these arguments could fit ecstatic utterances and many nontongue speakers accept this as a fact. However, these statements can also fit speaking in a foreign language that is not understood by the hearers. For example:

(1) One with the gift of language would be speaking only to God if neither he nor his hearers understood the language.

(2) One with this gift would be speaking by the power of the Holy Spirit since he had not learned the language through study. What he said would be both a mystery to him and his hearers since neither would understand the language (cf. I Cor. 14:13).

(3)—(4) If no one understood what he was saying, he cer-

---

[1]Jividen, Jimmy *Glossolalia—From God or Man?*, (Star Bible Publications, 1971), p. 41.

tainly would not be edifying anyone else. The only edifying he could do would be for himself by the knowledge that God was using him to speak a foreign language. The speaker's understanding would be unfruitful (I Cor. 14:14) if he were not able to translate the language in which he was speaking. This seems to be the case in many instances (cf. I Cor. 14:13).

(5) When Paul states that "no man understandeth" (I Cor. 14:2) he is not saying that no man living could understand the tongues or that they were mere jargon.

He means that no man present in the usual Corinthian assemblies understood them. Had speaking with tongues been mere hysterical "orgiastic" jargon, it certainly would not have bodied forth the mysteries of God, nor would it have edified the one speaking, nor could it have been interpreted by him or by others as Paul directs. Those who belittle the gift by construing it as a mere jargon approach dangerously near making Paul (and themselves likewise) criticize the Holy Spirit for giving such a senseless, abnormal gift. But those who read Paul correctly find that he is only censuring the *abuse* of the gift and not the nature of it.[1]

(6) If a brother were speaking in a tongue and a pagan came into the assembly who did not understand that language, he might well conclude that they were mad or insane.

Every argument that is used to identify the Corinthian tongues with ecstatic utterances also fits foreign languages which were not learned by the speaker and not understood by the hearers.[2]

2. Evidence for human languages. There is logical and weighty arguments that the tongue speaking in I Corinthians is the same as that found in the book of Acts.

Much confusion has been caused by some translators who inserted the word "unknown" in I Corinthians 14 (See 14:2, 4, 13, 14, 19, 27). It is in italics which means it is *not* in the original

---

[1] McGarvey, J. W. and Pendleton, Philip Y., *Thessalonias, Corinthians, Galatians and Romans,* (Standard Publishing Company, 1916), p. 135.

[2] Jividen, Jimmy, *Glossolalia—From God or Man?,* (Star Bible Pub., 1971), p. 43.

Greek. They inserted it in an effort to clarify the text. In this instance it has only confused it. The word "unknown" should not be in this chapter.

(a) Luke the companion of Paul wrote Acts (60-62 A.D.) after Paul had written I Corinthians (55-56 A.D.). Luke undoubtedly knew what was in I Corinthians either through reading it or by Paul's teaching. Paul would have known what Luke wrote in Acts since they were together in Rome while Luke was writing. It hardly seems possible that these two men would have written about two entirely different things and yet used the same word *glossa* to describe both events. Since foreign languages definitely were spoken in Acts, then foreign languages must have been spoken in Corinthians. If this is not so why did Luke not use different phraseology to indicate the difference? Lenski writes:

> Luke's description as given in the Acts is decisive for what Paul writes in Corinthians. This is reversed by some. They seek to determine what happened in Corinth and then either square Luke's account with what they think occurred at Corinth or posit two different gifts of tongues. Luke is the one who fully describes what the tongues are while Paul takes for granted that his readers know what they are and therefore offers no description. Luke writes for a reader (Theophilus) who may never have heard of this gift, at least may never have seen this gift in operation. Paul writes for readers who have often heard members of their own congregation speak in tongues.[1]

This makes sense. The tongue speaking in Corinth should be understood in the light of Acts and not in the opposite way.

If a word is used to describe a practice in the New Testament, it should always be taken to mean the same thing in other places unless the new context will not allow it.[2]

---

[1]Lenski, R. C. H., *Interpretation of I and II Corinthians*, (Wartburg Press, 1937), p. 504-505.

[2]Jividen, Jimmy, *Glossolalia—From God or Man?*, (Star Bible Pub., 1971), p. 38.

(b) In dealing with the purpose of tongues, Paul quotes from Isaiah (28:1-12): "In the law it is written, By men of strange tongues and by the lips of strangers will I speak unto this people; and not even thus will they hear me, saith the Lord" (I Cor. 14:21). This prophecy dealt with the invasion of Israel and Judah by the Assyrian nation (II Kings 17-18). Isaiah is saying that if the Hebrews do not listen to God's voice and repent, then they would have to listen to the foreign languages of their conquerors. The point here is that Isaiah is talking about a definite language—the Assyrian language. In verse 22 immediately following this quotation, Paul uses the word tongue as referring to the speaking in Corinth. It is the same Greek word *glossa* that is used in verse 21. If the word means foreign language in verse 21, it should also mean foreign language in verse 22.

(c) Paul indicates in I Corinthians 14:5 that the speaking in tongues could edify the church if it were properly translated. This would point to the conclusion that what was said was intelligent language that could be translated. This would be true of a normal, human language.

II. THE PURPOSE FOR THE GIFT OF TONGUES

There are four purposes for the gift of tongues given in the New Testament.

A. *Confirmation of the word.* The first purpose for spiritual gifts which included the gift of tongues was the confirmation of the Gospel of Christ. Jesus said: "and these signs shall accompany them that believe: in my name shall they cast out demons; *they shall speak with new tongues;* they shall take up serpents, and if they drink any deadly thing, it shall in no wise hurt them; they shall lay hands on the sick, and they shall recover" (Mark 16:17-18). Mark records that this promise was fulfilled: "And they went forth, and preached everywhere, the Lord working with them, and *confirming the word by the signs that followed*" (Mark 16:20).

This does not mean that every believer could do these things but rather that these are five of the miracles which were used to confirm the word preached. We find four of these occurring in

124

Acts (Acts 5:15-16; Acts 2:1-4; Acts 28:1-6; and Acts 19:11). The only one not mentioned in Acts is the drinking of poison.

Further proof for the confirming power of spiritual gifts is in Hebrews: "how shall we escape, if we neglect so great a salvation? which having at the first been spoken through the Lord, was confirmed unto us by them that heard; God also bearing witness with them, both by signs and wonders, and by manifold powers, and *by gifts of the Holy Spirit,* according to his own will" (Heb. 2:3-4). Please note that the writer says the message *"was* confirmed" not *"is being* confirmed." He indicates that the message of the gospel had already been confirmed and established by the time of the writing of Hebrews. S. Lewis Johnson wrote:

The gift of tongues is the gift of speaking in a known language for the purpose of confirming the authenticity of the message to the apostolic church.[1]

B. *Edification.* Paul states in I Corinthians 14:12, that the purpose for any spiritual gift was edification. In verse 26, he says "that all things be done unto edifying." In I Corinthians 14:5 Paul implies that tongues when translated or interpreted was for edifying. This is a second purpose.

C. *A sign of the Baptism in the Holy Spirit.* It is obvious from both Pentecost and Cornelius that the gift of tongues was one of the main evidences for the Baptism in the Holy Spirit. It was not the only one but it was a main one. This is a third purpose.

D. *A sign to Israel concerning the Messiah and His gospel.* There is considerable evidence to indicate that the gift of tongues may have had a special significance and meaning for the Jewish nation. Paul indicates in I Corinthians 14:21-22 that tongues or languages were a sign to Israel in the past (Isa. 28:11-12), and implies that the same was true in New Testament times.

It is significant that of the three occasions of speaking in tongues in the book of Acts, that two of them definitely apply to the Jews and the other may well have been. For example, on

---

[1]Gromacki, Robert G., *The Modern Tongues Movement,* (Presbyterian and Reformed Publishing Company, 1967), p. 105.

125

Pentecost the gift of tongues was used to convince the Jews that this phenomena was of God. In the house of Cornelius, the baptism in the Holy Spirit and the gift of tongues was for the purpose of convincing Peter and the six Jews that accompanied him that God had accepted the Gentiles, and so must they. The only questionable example is the tongue speaking at Ephesus. The implication seems to be that the twelve men were Jews, since they were disciples of John the Baptist. If this be true, then the gift of tongues could very well have been for the purpose of convincing them that what Paul had preached to them concerning Christ was true. This purpose is not so clear in Corinth but it certainly seems to be a purpose in the book of Acts.

III. SHOULD CHRISTIANS EXPECT THE GIFT OF TONGUES TODAY?

Paul states in I Corinthians 13:8: "whether there be tongues, they shall cease." Paul does not state exactly when but we believe that they ceased by the second century A.D. The following evidence is presented in proof of this point:

A. *The need for the gift ceased.* The main purpose for which the gift of tongues was given was to confirm the revelation of God (See Mark 16:17, 20; Heb. 2:3-4). Once a fact has been established and confirmed, it does not need to be confirmed in each generation.

When the Supreme Court establishes a certain principle of law, other courts do not have to reconfirm that. They simply refer to it as an established fact.

The Hebrew writer speaking of the gospel says that it "was confirmed unto us by them that heard" (Heb. 2:3). Note that he says that it was already confirmed at the time of the writing of Hebrews. The gospel does not need miraculous powers to confirm it today. It just needs to be preached.

B. *The means of imparting these gifts are not present today.* The gift of tongues was given in two ways: first, it accompanied the baptism in the Holy Spiriti (Acts 2:1-4; Acts 10:44-46). Second, it was imparted by the laying on of the Apostles' hands (Acts 19:1-6).

The Baptism in the Holy Spirit was given twice, to the Apostles on Pentecost, and to the household of Cornelius (Acts

126

2; Acts 10). The Baptism in the Holy Spirit was never promised to any others. There is no record of it being received by others. It was an initiatory act on Pentecost and was given when the Jews were initiated into the church. At Caesarea the baptism was given when the Gentiles were initiated into the Lord's church. There is no reason to expect this miraculous outpouring today. By the same token we do not expect the gift of tongues which accompanied the baptism in the Spirit.

It is quite obvious that the Apostles are not here today to impart the gift of tongues. The person claiming this gift today must explain how he has received it contrary to the way it was received in the New Testament.

C. *The gift of tongues was needed in the infancy of the church.* In I Corinthians 13:11, Paul implies that these special helps were to assist the church in its infancy. But that as a child lays aside his toys when he becomes a man, even so should these special helps be laid aside for the mature graces of faith, hope, and love (I Cor. 13:13).

D. *The gift of tongues has not been promised to us today.* There is no promise in the New Testament that we are to receive it. We are not told to expect it nor to make any effort to obtain it. In New Testament times Paul states that the Spirit distributed these gifts as He willed (I Cor. 12:11). God made the decision as to whether He gave them and to whom He gave them. This leaves it entirely within God's will and wisdom.

We would not be so brash as to say that God could not give men these miraculous gifts today. God has the right to do anything He wishes. It is within God's power to bring these miraculous gifts back to the church if His wisdom so dictates. All we are saying is that as far as we can see from the New Testament, the need for the gift of tongues has ceased and the means of imparting them has also ceased. Since God has not given any direct promise, then we do not expect them. Before we would conclude that God has restored this gift to the church today, we would ask for clear proof that this gift is of God and not from some other source.

Paul said: "tongues shall cease" (I Cor. 13:8). We believe they have.

REVIEW QUESTIONS—GIFT OF TONGUES

1. List the three cases of tongue speaking in Acts.

   a. _____

   b. _____

   c. _____

2. What was tongue speaking in Acts? _____

   _____

3. Give three proofs that the gift of tongues in the New Testament was human language.

   a. _____

   b. _____

   c. _____

4. List three purposes for the gift of tongues.

   a. _____

   b. _____

   c. _____

5. White three proofs that the gift of tongues is not present today.

   a. _____

   b. _____

   c. _____

XII

WORSHIP

I. Words Translated Worship.
   A. Hebrew.
   B. Greek.
   C. English word "worship".

II. Worship in the Old Testament.
   A. Altar.
   B. Temple.
   C. Synagogue.

III. Christian Worship.
   A. Different ways to worship.
   B. The elements of corporate worship.

IV. Worship In Spirit and In Truth.
   A. In truth.
   B. In spirit.

V. The purpose for Worship.
   A. Isaiah saw the Lord in all His Majesty and Holiness.
   B. Isaiah then comprehended his own sinfulness.
   C. Isaiah received forgiveness and strength to live for God.
   D. Isaiah was challenged to commit his life to God's service.

WORSHIP

I. WORDS TRANSLATED WORSHIP

A. *Hebrew.* The principal Hebrew word in the Old Testament for worship is *Shahah* meaning to "depress, bow down, prostrate oneself." Like Israel when they received word that God had sent Moses to lead them from Egypt, they "bowed their heads and worshipped" (Ex. 4:31; cf. Gen. 24:52, 27:29). This word is used 95 times in the Old Testament. It expresses a physical act as well as describing the attitude of mind and will toward God. It expresses the honor, reverence, and homage paid to superior beings; sometimes referring to men, but mostly to God.

B. *Greek.* The main Greek word in the New Testament for worship is *proskuneo,* meaning "to prostrate onself before the deity or a ruler". It is "used to designate the custom of prostrating oneself before a person and kissing his feet, the hem of his garment, the ground, etc.; the Persians did this in the presence of their deified king, and the Greeks before a divinity or something holy."[1] This word is used 59 times in the New Testament. An illustration of its use is I Corinthians 14:25: "He will fall down on his face and worship God." Like its Hebrew equivalent *(shahah) proskuneo* may be used for homage paid to men or to God. The idea of bodily prostration is less prominent in the New Testament, and the idea of humble submission of mind, soul and body is emphasized.

Another Greek word for worship is *latreuo* meaning "serve" in the sense of carrying out religious duties. This is Paul's idea in Acts 24:14: "But this I confess unto thee, that after the way which they call a sect, so *serve* (KJV—worship) I the God of our fathers. . ." This word is used 11 times in the New Testament.

C. *English word "worship".* The modern word worship comes from the Old English word *weorthscipe.* It is a combination of two words *weorth* meaning "worthy," and *scipe* meaning "shape, condition, or quality", so that the word originally meant "the condition of being worthy." Worship is giving honor, adoration, thanksgiving, and praise to God, who is worthy.

II. WORSHIP IN THE OLD TESTAMENT

There are four stages in the development of worship in the Bible: (1) The worship of the Patriarchs about the primitive altars (Gen. 12:7-8; 13:4); (2) Organized worship in the Taber-

---

[1]Arndt, W. F., Gingrich, F. W., *A Greek-English Lexicon of the New Testament and Other Early Christian Literature,* (The University of Chicago Press, 1957), p. 723.

nacle, and later in the Temple, with a complex ritual and system of sacrifices; (3) Synagogue worship; and (4) Christian worship in the New Testament.

A. *Altar.* The place of worship for the Patriarchs was the altar. These altars consisted of a mound of earth or a pile of unhewn stones. They had no fixed shape, but varied with the materials used. The altar might consist of a single rock or large stone (Judges 13:19; I Sam. 14:33-35), or a number of stones (I Kings 18:31f). They were built on high places, with a ramp up to them. Steps were forbidden for purposes of modesty (Ex. 20:26). The worship at these altars might consist of animal sacrifice (Gen. 8:20) or a simple act like Jacob's pouring oil on the rock in worship of Jehovah (Gen. 28:18; 35:14).

These altars are sometimes called "lay altars" since any Israelite could build one and offer certain sacrifices without the assistance of a priest. Moses gave instructions as to the materials and use of these altars (Ex. 20:24-26).

The Tabernacle and the Temple had altars that were different from the "lay altars". They were called "horned altars", because of the horns of bronze or copper on the corners. They were ministered to by priests.

The first altar mentioned in the Old Testament was the one built by Noah after the flood (Gen. 8:20). Subsequent altars were built by Abraham (Gen. 12: 7-8; 13:4, 18; 22:9), Isaac (Gen. 26:25), Jacob (Gen. 35:1-7), Moses (Ex. 17:15), and Joshua (Josh. 8:30-31). The importance of these altars is seen in that the word "altar" is used 433 times in the Bible (King James Version).

B. *Temple.* The second development in the worship in the Old Testament was the Tabernacle, later superceded by the Temple. The worship now became national instead of individual. The Jews assembled in great numbers to worship God (I Chron. 29:20). The temple was the center of the religious life of ancient Israel. The Psalms abound in references to it(42:4; 66:13, 84:1-4; 122:1, 9). Jews from all over the Mediterranean world flocked to Jerusalem to worship (Ps. 122:1-4; Acts 2:5-11).

In this public national worship the devout Jew found his greatest delight. In it were "interwoven together, his patriotism, his sense of brotherhood, his feeling of solidarity, his personal pride and his personal piety."[1]

Here the Jew participated in the great sacrifices in the temple, the ceremonial acts of reverence and intercession. He joined in the praises to Jehovah led by the Levite singers and musicians. During the feasts (Passover, Pentecost, Tabernacles, etc.) the Jew relived the great moments of his nation's history and taught his children of God's mighty acts and mercy. On the Day of Atonement he joined in the national penitence and seeking of God's forgiveness. Prayer was a vital part of worship in the temple.

C. *Synagogue.* The latest development in group worship in the Old Testament was the synagogue. The synagogue (literally "gathering-place", or "place of assembly") was the name applied to the Jewish place of worship in later Judaism and outside Palestine. It is supposed to have originated during the Babylonian Exile. In an effort to keep alive the worship of Jehovah, the Jews in Babylon met together to read the Law and to teach it to their children.

When the Jews returned to Palestine, they enjoyed the synagogue service so much, that they kept it and built synagogues in Palestine. During the time of Jesus there were synagogues in every major town or city. (Ten families could start one.) They continued to worship in the Temple also.

The appeal of the Synagogue was its informality, and emphasis on the study of the Old Testament. The services were simple, presided over by a man called a ruler, or elder. It became the educational and social center of the community as well as the religious center. It was a tremendous force in teaching the Jews as well as spreading the teaching of Jehovah to the Gentiles.

The synagogue service consisted in the recitation of the Jewish creed or Shema, "Hear, O Israel: Jehovah our God is one Jehovah. . ." (Deut. 6:4), followed by a ritual prayer, and concluding with a period of silent prayer by the people. Then a reader read the scriptures, some from the Pentateuch and some from the prophets. A sermon followed the scripture. The service

[1]*The International Standard Bible Encyclopaedia.* Edited by James Orr, (Wm. B. Erdmans Publishing Co., 1957), Volume V, p. 3111.

was closed with a blessing, if a priest were in attendance, if not, a prayer was substituted for the blessing.

The synagogue was a transition between the elaborate ritualism of the temple service and the simple but meaningful worship of the Church. The synagogue furnished the Lord's apostles and preachers a place to speak and was a great help in preparing the Gentiles for Christianity by the teaching of the one true God. Let us now examine the worship of the Church.

III. CHRISTIAN WORSHIP

Man was created to worship and glorify God—"every one that is called by my name, and *whom I have created for my glory. . ."* (Isa. 43:7). Peter writes: "But ye are an elect race, a royal priesthood, a holy nation, a people for God's own possession, *that ye may show forth the excellencies of him* who called you out of darkness into his marvellous light" (I Peter 2:9). Viewing the Christian as a priest worshipping God, Peter writes: "ye also, as living stones, are built up a spiritual house, to be a holy priesthood, *to offer up spiritual sacrifices,* acceptable to God through Jesus Christ" (I Peter 2:5; Heb. 13:15-16; Phil. 4:18). This involves the surrender of the entire life to God through Christ. Every act, and thought of the Christian should be worship. "WHATSOEVER ye do, in word or in deed, do all in the name of the Lord Jesus, giving thanks to God the Father through him" (Col. 3:17; cf. I Cor. 10:31). How is this to be done?

A. *Different Ways to Worship.* For purpose of clarification, worship can be divided into at least three categories: (1) Private devotions, (2) Corporate worship, and (3) Daily service.

1. Private Devotions. This primarily means prayer and Bible study. In prayer the Christian speaks to God. Through the Word, God speaks to man. Man brings his praise and thanksgiving to God through prayer. He adores the One who has given him "richly all things to enjoy" (I Tim. 6:17). As he meditates on the Word, he is paying reverence and homage to Him whose Will this book contains. Here the soul is bared to its Creator for forgiveness and comfort and strength. This warm, personal communion between saint and Saviour can be the sweetest and richest of worship.

133

Jesus enjoyed and practiced private prayer and meditation. Mark writes: "And in the morning, a great while before day, he rose up and went out, and departed into a desert place, and there prayed" (Mark 1:35; cf. Luke 5:16; 6:12; Matt. 14:23). He set the example for us!

2. Corporate Worship. The word "corporate" has reference to a body of persons united for some purpose. In this case it refers to the church assembled for worship. The New Testament teaches corporate or public worship. Luke records: "And they continued stedfastly in the apostles' teaching and fellowship, in the breaking of bread and the prayers" (Acts 2:42). This was the public or corporate worship of the church (Acts 20:7).

All worship in the New Testament is Christ centered, as well as God directed. It centered upon God's saving work in Jesus Christ. For example, the church met on the first day of the week, the Lord's Day to worship (Rev. 1:10). This was the day of Christ's resurrection. The Lord's Supper was the focal point of the worship—reminding them that Jesus loved them and gave Himself for them. They prayed to the Father in the name of Jesus (John 15:13-14; 16:24). If someone came to confess Christ and be baptized, then the church witnessed the drama of Christ's death, burial, and resurrection (Rom. 6:1-5).

3. Worship through daily service. The body of the Christian belongs to God the same as the soul. Paul said: "Present your bodies a living sacrifice, holy, acceptable to God, which is your spiritual (or reasonable) service (worship)" (Rom. 12:1). The body is the temple of the Holy Spirit, and can be used to serve God the same as the mind and spirit.

Real worship is the offering of everyday life to God. Real worship is not something which is transacted in a church; real worship is something which sees the world as the temple of the living God, and every common deed an act of worship. As Whittier wrote:

For he whom Jesus loved hath truly spoken
    The holier worship which He deigns to bless,
Restores the lost, and binds the spirit broken,
    And feeds the widow and the fatherless.[1]

---

[1]Barclay, William, *The Letter To The Romans,* The Westminister Press, 1957), p. 169.

134

In the parable of the Sheep and the Goats, the basis for acceptance or rejection was whether or not they had fed the hungry, given drink to the thirsty, clothed the naked, helped the sick, and visited those in prison. This is true worship the same as meeting about the Lord's Table on the Lord's Day. Benevolent works alone will not save. But none can be saved without these fruits of faith and love (cf. John 15:1-8; Isa. 58:6-8). A person will say, "I am going to church to worship God." He should also say, "I am going to the office, the mill, the mine, the school, the field to worship God."

Paul exhorts: "Whether therefore ye eat, or drink, or whatsoever ye do, *do all to the glory of God*" (I Cor. 10:31).

B. *The elements of corporate worship.* Acts 2:42 lists four elements of the church's worship: Apostles' teaching, fellowship, breaking of bread, and prayers.

1. Apostles' Teaching. The teaching was done orally by the inspired Apostles in the early years of the church. Later they wrote down their teaching and we have it in the New Testament. This teaching is the spiritual food for the Christian's soul, because it is the Word of God (John 6:53, 63). When we study the Word of God with reverence for the Author, striving to learn and obey His will, we are worshipping.

2. Fellowship. The word means "sharing", "communion", or "participation in". They shared their lives together in the church. They shared their material blessings (Acts 4:32-34; Rom. 15:26); their joys and sorrows (Acts 5:40-42; Rom. 12:15); their faith, work, and love. It was a tremendous sharing fellowship. This is worship as we glorify God the Father, by living and working together as His children.

3. Breaking of Bread. This refers to the Lord's Supper. Luke states that they continued "stedfastly" (constantly) in this as well as the other parts of public worship. Acts 2:46, may mean that the church ate the Lord's Supper daily for a while. After the church was fully established, the Holy Spirit seems to have directed the church to weekly worship which included weekly Communion. This is proven in Acts 20:7, where it states: "And upon the first day of the week, when the disciples came together *to break bread,* Paul preached unto them. . . ."

135

Most Christian leaders throughout history have believed that the Bible teaches weekly communion. For example, John Calvin wrote: "Let us remark, that the Lord's Supper might be most properly administered, if it were set before the church very frequently, and at least once in every week . . ."[1] Jonathan Edwards later wrote: "It seems plain by the Scripture, that the primitive Christians were wont (accustomed) to celebrate this memorial of the sufferings of their dear Redeemer every Lord's Day: and so I believe it will be again in the Church of Christ in days that are approaching."[1] Once a Christian has truly tried weekly communion he is not satisfied with anything less.

4. Prayers. Prayer, both private and public, is emphasized in the New Testament (Luke 18:1; I Thess. 5:17; I Tim. 2:1). Prayer was a vital part of the worship of the first Christians. It was also a key to their success (Acts 3:1, 4:23-31; 12:5; 14:23). In Acts 6:4, when the apostles listed their primary work as preaching and praying, they listed praying *first*. Prayer is the spiritual lifeline between earth and heaven. In prayer we adore God in thanksgiving and praise for His wonderful gifts, and through our petitions we acknowledge our need of Him. This is worship.

5. Singing. Praising God through song is not mentioned in Acts 2:42 as a part of the public, corporate worship. However, Ehesians 5:19 speaks of singing psalms, hymns, and spiritual songs. This could be either private or public worship and was undoubtedly both. Paul speaks of singing with the spirit and the understanding (I Cor. 14:15). Worshipping God through song was done in the Old Testament, it is being done in the Christian Age, and will be done in heaven (Rev. 5:9; 15:3-4). Obviously, this is pleasing to God who inspired the Psalmist to write: "Let the peoples praise thee, O God; let *all the peoples praise thee*" (Psa. 67:3).

6. Preaching. Preaching God's Word for the edification of His people is worship. It is for the preacher, and will be for the people if they listen humbly and obey what is preached. In Acts

---

[1]Calvin, John, *Institutes*, p. 703.
[1]Edwards, Jonathan, *Extract from Thoughts on Revival*, 1736—Quoted in *Plea*, (September, 1957).

136

20:7, the church met for the Lord's Supper, and Paul preached to them. Justin Martyr in describing the worship in his day (150 A.D.) states that after the reading the writings of the Apostles and Prophets, that the leader instructed the people and "exhorts to the imitation of these good things."[1] Teaching a lesson is also worship of God.

IV. WORSHIP IN SPIRIT AND IN TRUTH

A. *In Truth.* (John 4:24). To worship "in truth" is to worship according to the truth of God's Word. Since God is the one we worship, He has a right to prescribe how it should be done. If we expect to please Him, we must follow His instructions.

B. *In Spirit.* (John 4:24). This has a three-fold meaning. First, since "God is a Spirit" (literally "God is Spirit"—John 4:24), we must worship Him as Spirit—the original Spirit, and one from whom all spirits come (Acts 17:28; Psa. 135:15-18).

Secondly, we worship Him with our spirits (Rom. 1:9). A man is a spirit dwelling in a physical body. The real person, or spirit of man, is composed of the mind, emotions, and will or decision making power. Worship must then be a conscious, intelligent action (I Cor. 14:15). When one worships with the mind, emotions and will—this is worshipping with one's spirit.

Thirdly, we worship God with the aid of the Holy Spirit. Paul wrote: "For we are the circumcision (Jews), who worship by the *Spirit of God*. . ." (Phil. 3:3). He wrote the Ephesians: "For through him (Jesus) we both have our access *in one Spirit* unto the Father" (Eph. 2:18).

The Holy Spirit is especially helpful in prayer (Rom. 8:26). Paul exhorts: "praying at all seasons *in the Spirit*" (Eph. 6:18). May we thank God for the power of the Holy Spirit which enables us to worship acceptably.

V. THE PURPOSE FOR WORSHIP

The purpose for true worship is perhaps best illustrated in

---

[1]Moxe, A. Cleveland, *The Apostolic Fathers with Justin Martyr and Irenaeus.* "Weekly Worship of the Christians," Chapter LXII, p. 185-186.

the story of Isaiah's worship experience in the temple (Isa. 6:1-8).

A. *Isaiah saw the Lord in all His Majesty and Holiness.* In the vision, Isaiah "saw the Lord sitting upon a throne, high and lifted up" (Isa. 6:1). He was made aware of God's presence and power. He realized His holiness when the seraphim sang: "Holy, holy, holy, is the Lord of hosts" (Isa. 6:3-KJV).

Amidst this vision of kingly majesty and holiness, Isaiah's eyes could not linger on the divine face but fell instinctively to the train or long flowing robes which covered the floor or "filled the temple." Isaiah then looked at the heavenly creatures, the seraphim which surrounded the throne. They had six wings. Two wings were used to cover the face to screen it from the unbearable brightness of the divine presence (cf. Ex. 3:6; I Kings 19:13). One pair of wings was used to modestly cover the feet (probably meaning the body), from the divine eye (Ex. 20:26; 28:42f). They flew with the third pair of wings. Isaiah knew he was in the presence of the Lord.

The first purpose for worship is: To make the worshipper aware of the Presence, Power, and Perfection of God. Through the Lord's Supper the Christian is to discern the Lord's body and be fully conscious of His presence (I Cor. 11:29).

B. *Isaiah then comprehended his own sinfulness.* When the prophet saw God clearly, he then looked at himself. He did not like what he saw. He cried out, "Woe is me! for I am undone; because I am a man of unclean lips, and I dwell in the midst of a people of unclean lips." Then he tells why he feels that way—"for mine eyes have seen the King, Jehovah of hosts!" (Isa. 6:5). No man will ever see himself truly as he is, until he first sees God as He is.

The vision of God brought humility and repentance to Isaiah. He saw that he was sinful like other men. He was not as great, nor as good as he had thought.

The second purpose for worship is: To help man see himself as he is—a sinner who needs God's forgiving grace. This brings humility and repentance.

C. *Isaiah received forgiveness and strength to live for God.* When Isaiah cried out in confession and repentance, one of the seraphim flew through the temple to the great altar where the fire burned. With tongs it took a live coal from the fire and touched it to the prophet's lips and said, "Lo, this hath touched thy lips; and thine iniquity is taken away, and thy sin forgiven" (Isa. 6:7). When Isaiah saw himself and repented he was forgiven and strengthened.

A further purpose for Christian worship on the Lord's Day is to bring the believer to repentance and renewal before God. This means facing one's sins, and through repentance receiving the forgiveness of sin. Thus, cleansed and strengthened, he goes forth to serve Christ, knowing that the power and grace of God go with him.

D. *Isaiah was challenged to commit His life to God's Service.* Worship that does not result in greater service to God has failed in its final purpose. With a true vision of God, and having been purified from sin, Isaiah is now ready to hear and understand God's will. He hears God saying, "Whom shall I send, and who will go for us?" (Isa. 6:8). Immediately, Isaiah volunteers, "Here am I; send me!" (Isa. 6:8).

True worship ends in commitment of life. Worship is not working for God. It is like eating a nourishing meal in preparation for work. It is a spiritual "filling station", where the Christian is filled, strengthened, and challenged to go into the harvest field and reap for the Master.

When the church learns to *Worship* God and Christ acceptably, then it will be ready to *work* for God and Christ acceptably.

REVIEW QUESTIONS—WORSHIP

1. What is worship? _____

_____.

2. List the four stages in the development of worship in the Bible.

   a. _____

   b. _____

   c. _____

   d. _____

3. Man was created to _____ and _____ God.

139

4. List three ways to worship God: a. _____

   b. _____, c. _____.

5. Explain these statements:

   a. "Worship in Spirit" _____

   _____

   b. "Worship in Truth" _____

   _____

6. List three things to be accomplished in worship.

   a. _____.

   b. _____

   c. _____

BIBLIOGRAPHY

Arndt, William F., and Gingrich, F. Wilbur. *A Greek-English Lexicon of the New Testament.* University of Chicago Press, Chicago, 1957.

Barclay, William. *The Letter to The Romans.* (Philadelphia: Westminister Press, 1957.

Bittlinger, Arnold. *Gifts and Graces.* William B. Eerdmans Publishing Company, Grand Rapids, Michigan, 1968.

Boles, H. Leo. *The Holy Spirit—His Personality, Nature, Works.* Gospel Advocate Company, Nashville, Tennessee, 1942.

Book, William Henry. *The Columbus Tabernacle Sermons.* (Cincinnati: Standard Publishing Company).

Crawford, C.C. *Sermon Outlines on First Principles.* Dehoff Publications, Murfreesboro, Tennessee, 1961.

Crawford, C.C. *Sermon Outlines on the Cross of Christ.* Dehoff Publications, Murfreesboro, Tennessee, 1960.

DeWelt, Don. *The Power of the Holy Spirit, Volume I.* College Press, Joplin, Missouri, 1963.

Epp, Theodore H. *The Other Comforter.* The Good News Broadcasting Association, Inc., 1966.

Gromacki, Robert Glenn. *The Modern Tongues Movement.* Presbyterian and Reformed Publishing Company, Philadelphia, Pennsylvania, 1967.

Hasting, James, ed. *Dictionary of the Bible, Volume II.* (Charles Scribners Sons).

Horton, Wade H., ed. *The Glossolalia Phenomenon*. Pathway Press, Cleveland, Tennessee, 1966.

Hoven, Victor E. *Outlines of Biblical Doctrine*. Northwest Christian College Press, Eugene, Oregon.

Jividen, Jimmy. *Glossolalia—From God or Man?* Star Publications, Fort Worth, Texas, 1971.

Kellems, Jesse R. *The Resurrection Gospel*. (Standard Publishing Company, 1924).

Ketcherside, Carl W., ed. *Mission Messenger*, November, 1969.

Ketcherside, W. Carl, ed. *The Holy Spirit in Our Lives Today*. Mission Messenger, Saint Louis, Missouri, 1966.

Lenski, R.C.H. *The Interpretation of St. Paul's First and Second Epistle to the Corinthians*. Warburg Press, Columbus, Ohio, 1946.

McCrossan, T.J. *Speaking With Other Tongues—Sign or Gift—Which?* Christian Publications, Inc., Harrisburg, Pennsylvania.

McGarvey, J.W. *New Commentary on Acts of Apostles, Volume I*. (Cincinnati: Standard Publishing Company).

McGarvey, J.W., and Pendleton, Philip Y. *The Standard Bible Commentary—Thessalonians, Corinthians, Gelations and Romans*. (Cincinnati: Standard Publishing Company, 1916).

Milligan, Robert. *Scheme of Redemption*. (St. Louis: Christian Publishing Company).

Orr, James, ed. *International Standard Bible Encyclopedia*. William B. Eerdmans Publishing Company, 1957.

Robertson, A.T. *Word Pictures in the New Testament, Volume III & IV*. Broadman Press, Nashville, Tennessee, 1931.

Smith, Fred W., ed. *The Plea*, Steptember, 1957.

Smith, Wilbur M. *The Biblical Doctrine of Heaven*. Moody Press, Chicago, Illinois, 1968.

Young, Norvel. *20th Century Christian*, April, 1958.

A *fashionable* HISTORY *of* HATS & HAIRSTYLES

A FASHIONABLE HISTORY OF HATS &
HAIRSTYLES
was produced by

David West 👫 **Children's Books**
7 Princeton Court
55 Felsham Road
London SW15 1AZ

This edition first published in the United States in
2003 by Raintree, a division of Reed Elsevier, Inc.,
Chicago, Illinois.

For information address the publisher:
Raintree
100 N. LaSalle
Suite 1200
Chicago, IL 60602

Author: Helen Reynolds
Editors: Clare Hibbert, Marta Segal Block
Picture Research: Carlotta Cooper
Designer: Julie Joubinaux

Library of Congress Cataloging-in-Publication Data:
Reynolds, Helen, 1956-
  Hats and hairstyles / Helen Reynolds.
    p. cm. -- (A fashionable history of costume)
Summary: A historical look at hats and hairstyles.
Includes bibliographical references and index.
  ISBN 1-4109-0030-4 (lib. bdg.)
  1. Hats--Juvenile literature. 2. Hairstyles--Juvenile literature. [1.
Hats. 2. Hairstyles.] I. Title. II. Series.
  GT2110.R49 2003
  391.4'3--dc21
                              2002153952

ISBN 1-4109-0030-4

07 06 05 04 03
10 9 8 7 6 5 4 3 2 1

Printed and bound in China

PHOTO CREDITS:

Abbreviations: t-top, m-middle, b-bottom, r-right,
l-left, c-center.

The publisher would like to thank the following for
permission to reproduce photographs:
Front cover m, 3 & 10-11 – Mary Evans Picture
Library; br & 27br – Rex Features Ltd.; pages 4tr,
5tr, 6bl, 7l, 10tr, 11tr, 12bl, 13tr & br, 14tl & br,
16tl, 16-17, 17m, 20 all, 22l & tr, 23l & r, 24l,
25tl, 26tr & bl, 28tl, 28-29b – Mary Evans Picture
Library; pages 4br, 6br, 10l & br, 12br, 13bl, 14bl,
15l & bm, 16bm, 18bl, 18-19t, 22br, 26r – Dover
Books; pages 5tl & b, 6tr, 12tr, 16bl, 18tl, 21tr &
bl, 25bl, 27tl – The Culture Archive; page
7tr – ISG113867 A Young Lady of Fashion (oil on
panel) by Paolo Uccello (1397-1475), Isabella
Stewart Gardner Museum, Boston, Massachusetts,
USA/Bridgeman Art Library; pages 7br, 28-29t,
29mr – Hulton Archive; pages 8bl & tr, 8-9b, 9
both, 11bl & br, 15tr & mr, 17tl & tr, 19br, 21m
& br, 23tm, 24br, 25m & r, 26-27, 29bm – Rex
Features Ltd.; page 17mr – Karen Augusta,
www.antique-fashion.com; page 19tl, tm & tr –
Corbis Images; page28bl – Katz/FSP.

A *fashionable* HISTORY *of* HATS & HAIRSTYLES

Contents

BARBER'S POLE

A striped pole is the traditional sign for a barber's shop.

MEDIEVAL HATS

In the Middle Ages, rich European women wore towering hats draped with fluttering veils.

Hats & Hairstyles

Through the ages, hats and hairstyles have reflected not only the fashions of the day, but also a person's social status—and even religious beliefs. Head coverings offer protection and warmth, but they also mark a person's position in society. Until recently, ornate hairdos and hats were only for the rich. Most people wore practical hats and simple hairstyles.

Today, crowns and military berets still mark rank. However, hats and hairstyles are usually a fashion statement rather than a sign of status.

Victorian Advertisement
In the 1800s it was not fashionable to change hair color. However, many people resorted to dyes to cover greying hair.

Hats
The bicorn (c.1800) was a crescent-shaped man's hat. This picture also shows early top hats.

Hair History

Since early times, hairstyles have shown beauty and power. For example, the biblical warrior Samson made a holy vow not to cut his hair. He lost his strength when his hair was cut by Delilah. Haircuts and styles could also be a sign of status. Wealthy ancient Assyrians arranged their hair in fancy curls, while Egyptians shaved their heads and wore glossy wigs.

EGYPTIAN SIDELOCK

Egyptian nobles had shaved heads, but during their youth they kept one sidelock of long hair.

The long hair story

In ancient Greece and Rome, men kept their hair short, but the only women with short hair were slaves. Although fashions varied, noblewomen wore their long hair braided and knotted. They even used hair dye. In the late 1700s, there was a new European craze for classical styles following the discovery of the ruins of a Roman town in Pompeii, Italy.

CURLY STYLES

In the 1830s, women wore their hair in neat buns and chignons, with tight ringlets curling down at the sides. Curls were also fashionable for men.

ROMAN LADY

In ancient Rome, slaves styled their mistresses' hair. They used heated irons to create lots of tiny curls. These were held back from the face by hairpins of valuable ivory or bone.

TRADITIONAL JAPANESE COIFFURE

These Japanese court fashions of 1890 had changed little since the 1100s, when they were copied from the Chinese. Long hair was lacquered and then secured with elegant combs and hairsticks.

15TH-CENTURY SKINHEAD

Renaissance ladies shaved their hairline to achieve a high forehead. Hair, when not covered, was usually tied or plaited around the head.

Short cuts

Women's styles stayed long until around World War I (1914–1918). Then, the famous ballroom dancer Irene Castle (1893–1969) cut her hair in a boyish bob. By the 1920s, many young women were cutting their hair. The bob gave way to the shingle, which was cut even closer to the head.

BIRTH OF THE BOB

Movie star Louise Brooks (1906–1985) was one of the first famous women to go short. She wore a straight, sleek bob.

Alternative Styles

The bob was considered shocking when it first appeared, but to some of the young women who wore it, the style was about more than just fashion. It was a symbol of their equality to men. The bob reappeared during another period of freedom and change—the 1960s. Vidal Sassoon (1929–) brought out his five-point bob in 1964. As the decade progressed, young people began to see that how they dressed and how they wore their hair could express their individuality, identity, and the way they felt about society.

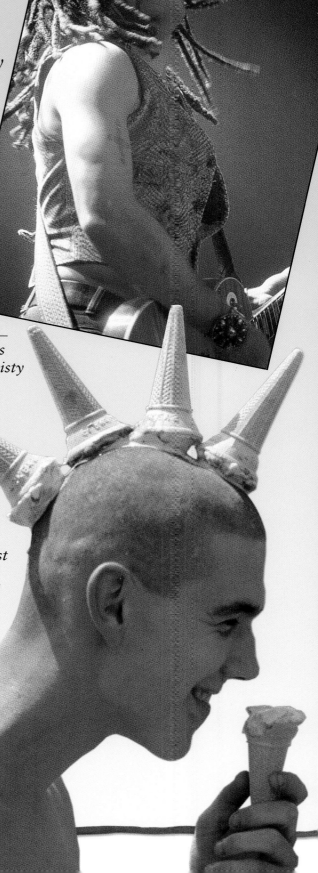

Lenny Kravitz

Kravitz (1964–) wears dreadlocks – long, twisty locks of matted hair.

Superhero Chic

Shaved heads can be made more funky and fun with motifs, created by clipping around a pattern.

Made to melt

Punk rockers liked to shock by styling their hair into an outlandish, spiky crest called a Mohawk. This man has created a sweet version—out of ice cream cones!

During the late 1960s, African Americans began to celebrate their identity through their hair. They stopped straightening their hair so it conformed to "white" styles. Followers of Rastafarianism grew their hair into long, matted dreadlocks. Other styles adopted to express black pride include the Afro and African-style braiding.

Young people often adopt a hairstyle to show they are part of a group. Close-cropped hair may be mainstream today, but the style was first worn by skinheads to express aggression. Punk rockers, too, used shocking styles to demonstrate their rejection of "normal" society and its values.

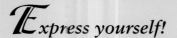

*A*WESOME AFRO

People of African origin, often have naturally curly, full-bodied hair, and the Afro emphasizes these qualities with pride. But although the style looks natural, it actually requires a lot of work. Strands of hair have to be teased out with a special Afro comb.

THE MULLET

Seen by most people today as tacky, the mullet was popular in the 1980s. It combined a short, clean-cut look in front with more free-spirited long hair in the back.

Wigs

Nobility in ancient Egypt wore wigs over shaved heads. Men's wigs were short and fringed, while women wore longer wigs of braided, twisted hair.

Wigging out

Wigs were popular with wealthy people in 17th-century Europe, too. People did not have hot running water in their homes, and dirty, greasy hair was a problem. Many men chose to shave their heads and wear wigs instead. Wigs were usually made of human, yak, or horsehair, and they came in a staggering range of styles—long or short, straight, curled, or frizzed. By the 1730s, some wigs were dusted with white wig powder that could be scented with orange blossom or lavender. The white, full-bottom wig worn by British judges dates from this period.

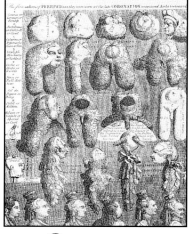

Costly choices

These wigs of the 1700s were expensive. Only the wealthy had several.

Nile style

Thick, glossy, black wigs were worn in ancient Egypt by the nobility. Some were ornately braided with gold and silver threads.

Wigmaking

Some 18th-century wigs were in natural colors, but the most fashionable were white. Many were tied in the back with a black ribbon.

The decline of the wig?

By 1800 wigs were no longer in fashion, although they were still worn by bald people. The most expensive wigs were made of human hair, and people could earn a lot of money by selling their hair. Today wigs are far less common. Many people who are bald from chemotherapy still wear wigs, and many others wear outrageous wigs as a fashion statement.

WIG CARTOON OF 1780

Wigs grew to enormous heights—and harbored all sorts of vermin!

POWDER PUFF

18th-century barbers were kept busy cleaning, curling, and powdering their clients' wigs. They also sold long wig scratchers made of ivory or bone. Men used these to scratch at the lice nits, or mice that often burrowed into their wigs!

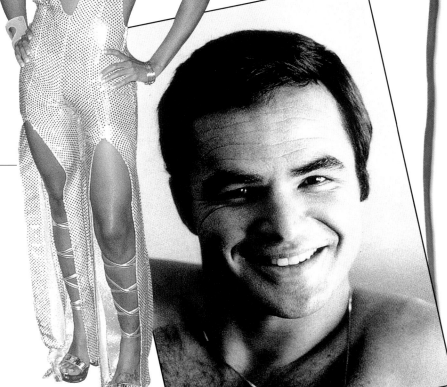

TOP TOUPEE

Actor Burt Reynolds (1936–) is famous for his toupees (hairpieces).

PARTY WIGS

Wigs are far more convenient than colored dyes for women who want a fun, party look. Pop star Lisa "Left Eye" Lopes (1971–2002) wore a bright green wig when she hosted the Music of Black Origin Awards in London.

All About Adornment

Elaborate hair decorations have been popular since ancient times. The Egyptians wove jewels into their wigs, while in ancient Greece and Rome women wore gold, silver, and jeweled hairbands. Some accessories were practical. Julius Caesar (100–44 B.C.E.) is said to have adopted the laurel wreath to cover his bald spot!

Sweet scents

The Egyptians sometimes placed cones of scented wax on top of their wigs. As the wax melted it dripped over the wig, making it look glossy—and smell wonderful!

Braids & nets

In 12th-century Europe, women either covered their hair or wore it in long, twisted braids. From the 1200s, women's hair was increasingly covered with a veil, mantle (hooded cloak), or headdress. From the 1400s, hair was worn loose with a circlet (a circle-shaped ornament), or braided and pinned into fillets (embroidered hairnets).

Geisha girl

Japanese geishas were known for their great beauty. They wore costly ornamental combs and hairpins called kanzashi.

Circlets & fillets

Early Renaissance women (c.1500s) brushed back their hair and pinned it. They wore circlets, fillets, and hairnets decorated with gold, silver, and jewels.

Curls, feathers, & combs

From the late 1700s, Greek-inspired ornaments were popular, worn with classical curls. Strips of cloth called bandeaux were wrapped around the head and sometimes finished with large feathers. By 1820 fashionable hair was often worn in a plaited knot, held in place with decorative hairpins and combs.

Tall plumes

In the 1790s, many women increased their height by wearing tall feathers in their hair —but some took the fashion too far!

Blooming Beauties!

In the early 1900s, women often used fresh or silk flowers as hair decorations. Maids were specially trained to pile the hair high and weave in lots of pretty blooms.

Evening bandeau

The bandeau made a comeback in the 1920s as a way to jazz up short styles. The jewelry company Cartier (founded in 1847) even designed bands of diamonds.

Religion & Ceremonies

Almost every religion has special forms of headwear, either worn as a constant reminder of faith, or worn only for religious ceremonies. Some Native Americans, for example, traditionally wear elaborate, feathered headdresses for their rituals. Royals have also been required to wear special headwear.

Crowns for kings & queens

Rulers in ancient Egypt and Assyria were probably the first to wear crowns. The Egyptian pharaoh wore a double crown to show that two lands—Upper and Lower Egypt—were united under his control. Since then, crowns have often been a symbol of supreme authority, worn by emperors, czars, and kings. The start of a ruler's reign is usually marked by a coronation, or crowning ceremony.

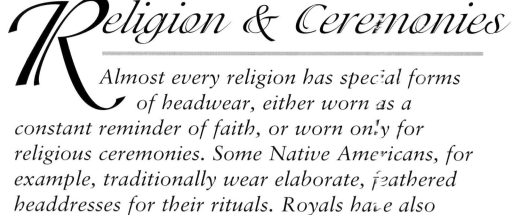

EGYPTIAN KING IN BATTLE

From 3100 B.C.E., pharaohs wore tall crowns to mark kingship. The battle crown, or khepresh, was usually made of leather. It was decorated with gold or bronze discs.

KINGLY CROWN

Medieval rulers wore gem-studded crowns of iron, bronze, silver or gold.

BISHOPS' MITERS

Bishops and archbishops wear tall, decorative hats called miters. They are shaped to point up to heaven.

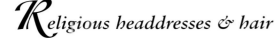

Religious headdresses & hair

Hats and hairstyles can be a sign of faith. Many Muslim women wear a headscarf called a hejab, while the men wear a prayer cap called a kufi. Orthodox Jews cover their heads, too. The men wear hats, but women wear either hats or wigs. Buddhist and Christian monks may shave their heads as a sign of humility before God.

The Sikh turban

To show their religious commitment, certain Sikhs wear the Five Ks. These are the kirpan (dagger), kangha (comb), kara (bangle), kaccha (pants), and kesh (uncut hair). The turban is not one of the Five Ks, but all Sikh males wear it to keep the kesh tidy.

Monk's tonsure

Monks shave their heads in a style called a tonsure. The circle of hair represents Jesus' crown of thorns.

The yarmulke

All Jewish men wear a skullcap called a kippah or yarmulke when they pray.

Nun's headdress

Some nuns wear a dark veil, held in place with a white band, or coif. A white wimple covers the throat.

Weather Protection

Long before they were fashion items, hats were worn for warmth or as defense from the elements. The ancient Greeks, for example, wore straw sunhats called petasos.

Fur & Feathers

19th century American fur trappers wore bear- or raccoon-skin hats to keep them warm in the mountains.

Rain or shine

Fur, felt, wool, and recently, synthetic fleece provide the best insulation against the cold. The first waterproof hats appeared in the 1800s. The sou'wester was a sailor's hat. It was made of rubber or oilskin, and it was specially shaped so any rainwater would run off the wide brim at the back.

Sunhats were very popular in the 1800s, as people prized their pale complexions. Womens' bonnets had wide brims to protect them from the sun. Men wore straw boaters. A hat cover, called a havelock, was worn by men in hot climates. It had a back flap to protect the neck.

Storm ahead!

Sou'westers were traditionally worn at sea. They are named after rain-bearing southwesterly winds.

Travel hats

Women traveling in the first, open-top cars wore motoring hats to protect their hair from the wind and dust.

Straw Boaters, 1930s

Boaters are stiff straw sunhats trimmed with a heavy, corded band, known as petersham ribbon. This advertisement is from the 1930s although the hats were popular with men since the late 19th century.

Made in the Shade

Popular in Spain and Mexico, the sombrero has an enormous brim that gives all-around shade from the sun.

Field Fashion

In Southeast Asia, workers are busy in the rice fields all day. They wear wide, veiled sunhats.

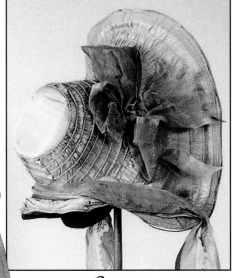

Clever collapsibles

Hats can be bulky to store, but some are designed to go flat. 19th-century ladies often wore a calash—a silk hood on a folding whalebone frame. The panama is a man's sunhat from South America. Even if it is rolled flat to fit in a suitcase, it will spring back to its original shape.

Sun bonnets

Poke bonnets were usually made of straw. The large poke, or front brim, protected the wearer's nose from sunburn.

Return of the hat!

When tans became fashionable in the 1920s, sunhats went out of fashion. However, recent worries about links between suntans and skin cancer have led to increased sunhat sales.

Sporty style

The baseball cap is now the most widely worn sunhat. It was popularized in the 1920s and 1930s by the baseball star Babe Ruth (1895–1948).

Helmets for Heroes

Helmets originally developed as battle dress and they kept the head safe from hard knocks. The style of a battle helmet was always very important, because it identified which side a soldier was on.

From horse skulls to haute couture

Ancient Ethiopian warriors are said to have worn horse skulls, complete with flowing manes, as helmets! However, most early helmets were made of leather or metal. Medieval knights wore steel helmets as part of their armor. Plate armor was strongest, but also extremely heavy. Chainmail was lighter and could withstand sword thrusts, but not showers of arrows. In the late 1960s, medieval chainmail made a high-fashion comeback when Spanish designer Paco Rabanne (1934–) brought out metal-linked mini dresses with matching helmets.

Hoplite's helmet

Greek hoplites (foot soldiers) had helmets of hammered bronze with horsehair crests. Their helmets were the first to have a nose shield.

Victorious gladiator

Gladiators fought to the death as entertainment for the ancient Romans. Some were equipped with limited armor, such as a helmet, sword, and shield.

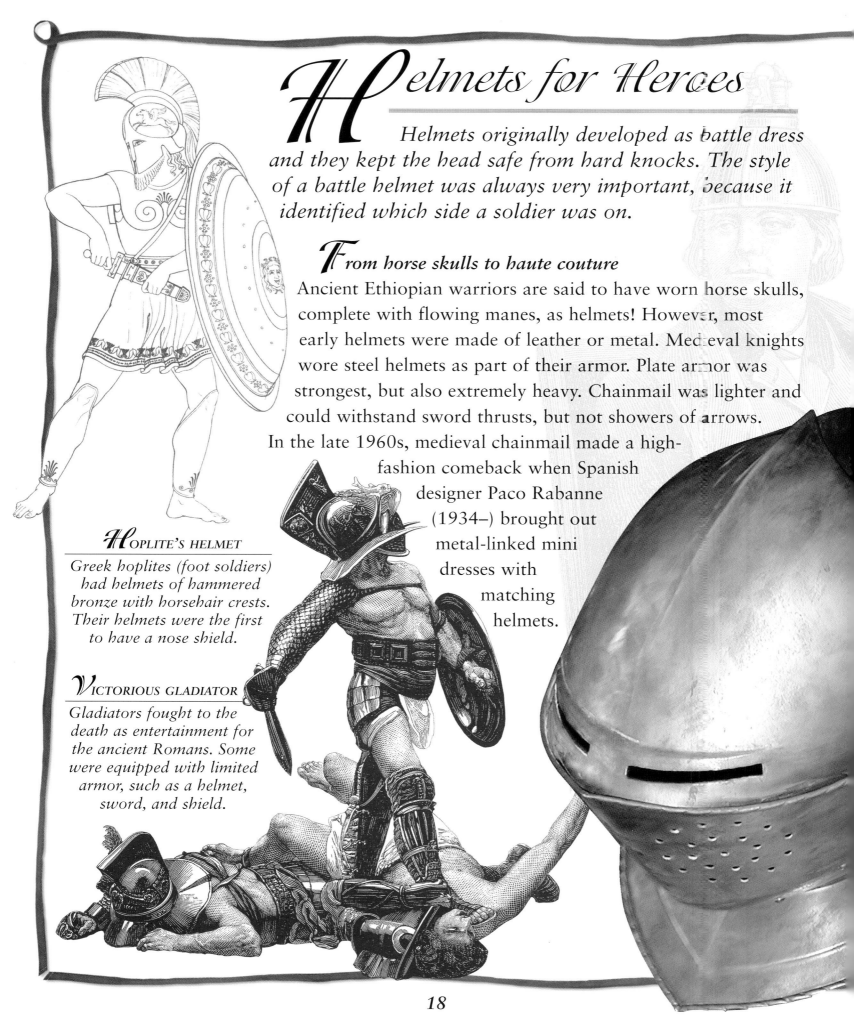

𝓗ARD HATS

Helmets protect construction workers' heads from falling masonry or machinery.

𝓗ELMETS FOR TODAY'S ARMED FORCES

A modern fighter pilot's helmet has a glare-free visor and easily hooks up to an oxygen supply. For soldiers on the ground (inset), helmets protect against bombs and bullets. Camouflage is all important.

𝓗ard-wearing, hard-working

Today soldiers wear helmets made of super-strong synthetic materials such as Kevlar. These offer more protection than ever before and are lightweight and easy to wear.

Protective helmets are also worn by police, firefighters, and workers on building sites. Motorcylists put on crash helmets to protect their heads, and jockeys wear reinforced riding hats in case they are thrown from their horses. Other sports where helmets are worn include cycling, skateboarding, ice hockey, baseball, and football.

𝓜EDIEVAL PLATE HELMET

Knights' helmets were usually made from steel. The hinged visor had eye slits and breathing holes. Helmets were sometimes engraved with family crests.

FOOTBALL PLAYERS

A cage at the front of Joe Montana's helmet protects his vulnerable nose and teeth from being broken.

Headscarves & Turbans

The classic headwrap is the Eastern turban, but Westerners were wearing similar head coverings more than a thousand years ago. For women, there was the coverchief, a square or semi-circle of linen that wrapped around the head and neck, leaving the face exposed. For men, there was the bourrelet, a roll of fabric worn under a hood called a chaperon.

High hood, 1300s

Medieval noblemen wore a turban-style hood called a chaperon. The headwrap underneath was called a bourrelet.

Gifts from the East

Eastern-style turbans became fashionable in the West during the 1700s when it became usual for rich young Europeans to travel. Some men adopted the headdresses of the places they visited, wearing the turban when relaxing at home. By the end of the century, turbans were part of women's evening dress. They were often decorated with ostrich plumes and sparkling jewels. French designer Paul Poiret (1879–1944) revived the look in 1909 when he created a collection of costumes inspired by the Middle East.

Ladies' headwraps

Medieval women wore a veil over their coverchief, or headwrap (c.1200s). Together called a wimple, it was secured with a circlet.

Cashmere and muslin turbans

Romantic poets such as Lord Byron (1788–1824) wrote about exotic places and often wore costumes to match. Women adopted turbans in fine fabrics too, as illustrated in 1833 (left)—perfect foils for the high, wide hairstyles.

Silken squares

The 20th century saw the rise of the headscarf. A practical item for women at work, the scarf became a fashion item during the 1950s. The Parisian saddle company Hermès (founded in 1837) produced expensive silk squares with horse motifs that were widely copied. Hermès scarves remain popular at high-society sports events; one famous customer of Hermés is Queen Elizabeth of England (1926–).

Chic sheiks on screen

Many movies from the 1920s featured Middle Eastern themes. Starlets and other fashionable women started wearing turbans and headscarves as a result.

War worker

This headscarf of 1943 was typical of women doing war work. It kept hair clean and safe from factory machinery.

Sporty!

In the 1950s, silk, satin, or nylon scarves were very fashionable as casual wear. The square scarf was folded in half to make a triangular shape and knotted under the chin.

Desert wrap

Kaffiyehs are headdresses worn by Arab men. They give protection against sandstorms and the strong desert sun.

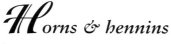all hats

In medieval Europe hats became very elaborate and ostentatious. Smooth, high foreheads were considered very elegant, so fashionable women pulled back their hair and wore tall hats for extra emphasis.

Horns & hennins

Twin turrets were added to the square wimple to create a horned headdress similar in style to the hats worn today by Dutch women as part of their national dress. In Europe, around 1450 a single-turret steeple-hat called a hennin was worn.

Crowning glories

In the early 1600s, a high-crowned, small-brimmed hat called the capotain was worn by both sexes. Even after it went out of fashion, the hat remained popular with the Puritans (Protestants who wanted Church reforms).

Medieval hats, 11th & 13th centuries

In the Middle Ages, noblewomen wore horned headdresses (with two turrets) and hennins (with a single steeple). Both were over 3 feet tall and draped with long gauzy veils.

High hat

Like Victorian British police headwear, this American policeman's hat of the early 20th century added height and offered protection.

Puritan in a sugarloaf hat

Puritans dressed plainly. They named their high-crowned capotains "sugarloaf hats," because they were cone-shaped, just like tall mounds of refined sugar.

Top Hat

The shiny silk top hat, pictured here in the 1800s, was first worn with both day and evening wear.

Truly a Ten-Gallon Hat?

Larry Hagman, of Dallas *fame*, often wears a ten-gallon hat, named after a Mexican hat with ten decorative braids. *Galón* is Spanish for "braid."

Bearskin Busby

This British guardsman wears a busby, or bearskin hat. Busbies were first worn by Hungarian cavalrymen as early as the 1400s.

Top notch

The 1800s saw the appearance of the most famous tall hat of all—the top hat. Made of silk plush, it was worn with formal day wear. After the bowler (or derby) became usual day wear, the top hat remained the *only* hat to wear with a dress suit. Probably the most famous top hat belonged to Fred Astaire (1899–1987), a dancer who even starred in a musical called *Top Hat* (1935).

Flat Hats

In the 1500s, men and women began to wear flatter hats. One close-fitting hat was the toque, which was usually brimless. Velvet berets, perhaps trimmed with fur, were also popular and were worn sloping to the side. In the 1600s hats stayed relatively flat but developed a broad brim that could be decorated with an ostrich feather.

Simple... & not-so-simple

As the hats worn by the nobility became wider and more ostentatious, Puritan women opted for plain, white linen caps. Similar caps were worn at home by ladies and gentlemen of the nobility for protection in drafty rooms. By the 1700s, these had developed into fancy boudoir (bedroom) or morning caps. They were worn by leisured women to cover rumpled or undressed hair.

PILLBOX

Pillbox hats (named for their shape) have been around since the 1930s. They were made popular in the 1960s by First Lady Jackie Kennedy. This "tilted" pillbox hat is from 1953.

Flatcaps for all

Flat, woolen caps are easy to produce and cheap. From the 1600s, they were worn for warmth by workers and apprentices. In the late 1800s, these developed a peak at the front. Flatcaps were no longer worn only by the working classes. Well-to-do people wore tweed ones for sports such as golf, while middle-class people wore them for cycling and hiking. However, gentlemen never wore a flatcap in town. During the 1960s fashionable young women wore flatcaps made of PVC (a synthetic material) or leather, after André Courrèges (1923–) teamed them with his catsuits and miniskirts.

Cute, Crocheted Caps

Knitting and crocheting were popular pastimes in the 1940s. Colorful caps could be crocheted using just a few leftover lengths of yarn.

The Beret

French workers wear a flatcap called a beret. It is also part of many soldiers' uniforms.

Tartan Tam-o'-Shanters

Versions of the Scottish tam-o'-shanter are popular with British soccer fans.

The Worker's Flatcap

In this 19th-century photograph, only the manual workers wear flatcaps. The cap became a symbol of the working class.

Outrageous Hats

For the last 50 years, it has no longer been necessary for men and women to wear hats when they go out. Today more than ever before, hats are worn only for special occasions, and designer hats can cost more than the rest of the outfit put together! Modern milliners delight in designing eye-catching creations. But, as with all forms of dress, outrageous hat fashions are not a new phenomenon.

Causing a sensation

Very often a hat style gradually becomes more extreme. That is how, in the 1800s, neat and simple bonnets grew into outsize fashion statements. Hatmakers often stick to the style and shape that is fashionable at the time, but then they exaggerate it to make the hat stand out.

Costume hat

This French postcard of the 1920s shows a cloche hat decorated with a huge spiderweb!

Silly strolling hats

Every era has its fashion victims. In the 1800s, men fell for top hats that stretched ever taller—while their wives wanted bonnets that spread out ever wider.

Taken to extremes

The poke bonnet's brim shaded the wearer, but it could be absurdly large.

Dazzling designers

The best milliners do more than rehash old ideas. They create wearable works of art that express the feelings of the time. One of the most imaginative was Elsa Schiaparelli (1890–1973). Her creations were inspired by Surrealism, an art movement that found beauty in the absurd.

Key designers since then include Simone Mirman (1920–), whose crazy, floppy hats captured the mood of the 1960s. In the 1980s, Graham Smith (1938–) made big, bold hats for power-dressing women. Since 1990 milliner Philip Treacy (1967–) has built a reputation for hats in amazing shapes!

SASSY SCHIAPARELLI

Schiaparelli's designs included hats shaped like shoes or lamb chops! She collaborated on these with Surrealist artist Salvador Dalí (1904–89).

HORSING AROUND

Horse races seem to inspire large hats. The cream of designer hats are worn to the British Ascot races and the Kentucky Derby. This hat was designed by David Shilling (1953–) and is worn by his mother.

TREACY HAT

Irish milliner Philip Treacy is known for his oversized sculptural designs. Many of his hats seem to twist up toward the sky. Treacy opened his own London hat shop in 1990.

Hat & Hair Technology

Although many hats are now made in factories, hat-making techniques have changed little over the centuries. Factory machines mimic the methods used by milliners.

How to...

The traditional way to make a felt or straw hat by hand is to use a hatter's block. This is made of wood or, more usually today, of aluminium. Felt and straw are the most commonly used hat materials. Both need to be mulled, or dampened with steam, so they will be easy to mold into shape on the hatter's block. The crown is shaped first, then the brim is added. Next, the hat is stiffened with a special gumlike solution, so that it will not lose its shape. Finally, the hat is trimmed with a band or ribbons.

Mad as a hatter

In the past, hatters used mercury salts for felt making, unaware it was poisonous. As a result, many hatters became ill with a mental disorder called erethism.

Top trims

Hats for special occasions are artistically trimmed with net veils, fake flowers, or huge bows of satin ribbon.

Advertisement

Wavy hair was fashionable in the 1920s and 1930s. To achieve the look, women could buy all sorts of gadgets.

SET YOUR O

YOU CAN SET YOUR WAVES
The BUTYWAVE WAVESETTER, designed by or of our hairdressers, will set your waves, exactly as they automatic—there are no "messy" proces strong or weak.

ADJUSTED IN A SECOND TO
The BUTYWAVE WAVESETTER can be adjust your hairdressing in a few seconds. Glance at the people it is. The pictures are actual photograph pressed gently into deep natural waves, which last wearing the BUTYWAVE WAVESETTER for 4

SO COMFORTABLE YOU CAN
The BUTYWAVE WAVESETTER has no m you've got it on it's so comfortable. complete comfort.

YOU SAVE MONEY TOO
Think! 5/- is all you have to pay for years convenience of periodical visits to the hairdress

5/- BUT
WAV

Obtainable from all high-class Drapers, Chem case of difficulty post coupon to the Bu

To The Butywave Co., 10 Tachbr
Dear Sir,—Please send me by
WAVING CAPS, for which I enc

NAME

$\mathcal{H}$air-raising wigs & transplants

Long ago, wigs were the only option for someone wishing to disguise baldness. Wigs can be made of real or synthetic hair. Most are mass-produced, but some are handmade for a perfect fit. The wig maker makes a net cap to fit the client's head, then tucks in tufts of hair with a hook-shaped needle. Each tuft is securely knotted by hand, and making a wig can take around 40,000 knots.

These days, some people choose a permanent, surgical remedy instead, with hair transplants.

$\mathcal{P}$LUG-IN HAIR

(Above) Here, a transplant surgeon fills a bald area with plugs (sections of scalp containing about 10 hairs). It takes several sessions to cover the average bald spot. Today full hair transplant operations can also be done.

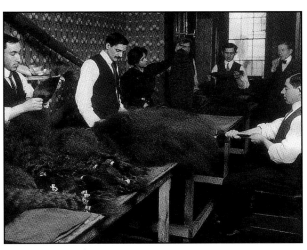

$\mathcal{W}$IG WORKERS IN NEW YORK

This is what a wig production line looked like 80 years ago. Employees made wigs by hand from human hair.

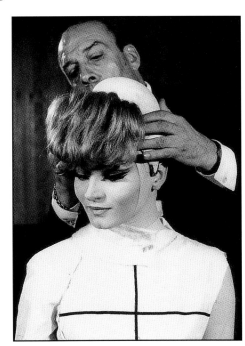

$\mathcal{F}$INAL FIT

Hairpieces, like this one from the 1960s, are expensive if made-to-measure. Ready to wear models are cheaper.

$\mathcal{H}$ats off to hair care

Hair fashions change as new inventions appear. In 1904, a German hairdresser demonstrated the permanent wave or perm, and soon curly styles became easier for everyone to achieve. Electric dryers, clippers, crimpers, curlers, and straighteners have all revolutionized how people style their hair. Sprays, gels, mousses, waxes, and other products also influence fashionable styles and will continue to do so.

Timeline

Prehistory
Early peoples may have cut their hair for special rites or cut it off when it got in the way of hunting. Fur hoods were worn for warmth.

The ancient world
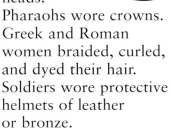
The ancient Egyptians wore glossy wigs over shaved heads. Pharaohs wore crowns. Greek and Roman women braided, curled, and dyed their hair. Soldiers wore protective helmets of leather or bronze.

The Middle Ages
In the 1100s, women covered their hair with a coverchief, shawl, or mantle. Royals and nobles wore crowns and coronets. From the 1200s, incredibly tall horned headdresses and steeple-hats were fashionable. Men's hair was cut short with a thick, round fringe. The fashionable man wore a bourrelet on his head, covered with a hood called a chaperon.

16th century
Men began to wear a stiff, felt cap. About 1530 the soft, halo-brimmed bonnet made an appearance. Toward the end of the century, noblewomen began to curl their hair and adorn it with jewels. Elizabeth I of England (1533–1603) set a trend for red hair and wigs.

17th century
Fashionable men at the turn of the century wore the tall-crowned capotain hat. This later became the Puritan's sugarloaf hat, which was worn over short hair. Puritan women wore simple caps. The nobility wore low-crowned, wide-brimmed hats over long, wavy hair. Ladies wore their hair in ringlets and a braided knot at the back.

18th century
For most of the 1700s, women frizzed and curled their hair with curling irons to create big styles that were often covered with pomade and white powder. The fashionable man wore a wig, topped with a three-cornered tricorn hat or, later, the two-cornered bicorn.

In the late 1700s, wigs were abandoned for a more natural look. Bandeaux, turbans, and ostrich feathers were popular evening headwear for women.

19th century
By 1840 women usually wore their hair in a bun, with ringlets framing the face. The poke bonnet was worn with wide-skirted dresses. Fashionable men wore top hats, while workers wore flat-caps. At the end of the century, women's hairstyles grew taller. Large hats became fashionable, too.

20th century & beyond
The permanent wave was invented by Karl Nessler in 1904, paving the way for wavy, short styles in the 1920s. Close-fitting cloche hats were worn by day, bandeaux in the evening. For men, the short-back-and-sides hairstyle became fashionable. In the 1930s, marcelling was popular. Women's hair was styled with the curling tongs invented by Marcel Grateau in the 1870s. During World War II (1939–1945), women adopted headscarves to protect the hair from dirt and machinery. In the 1950s the full, bouffant hairstyle became popular with women, but required weekly setting at the salon. It developed into the tall beehive styles of the early 1960s. Then, Vidal Sassoon invented his low-maintenance bob that only required cutting every six weeks and was widely copied. In the late 1960s and the 1970s hippy fashions arrived; men and women wore their hair long. Street styles, such as Mohawks, were fashionable with the young. The designer hat became popular for special occasions. Since the 1990s, young men—and some women—have favored short, cropped styles. Spray-on dyes and hair extensions have also offered more flexibility for people wanting to change their look in an instant.

Glossary G

bandeau strip of decorative cloth that is wrapped around the head, usually for evening wear

bouffant full, puffed-out hairstyle popular during the 1950s

brim edging around a hat that projects over the head and face

cap hat without a brim, or with a very small brim or visor at the front

chignon (pronounced sheen-yon) soft bun or coil of hair worn at the back of the neck

coif (pronounced kwaff) close-fitting cap, or the band at the front of a nun's headdress

coiffure (pronounced kwaff-yur) hairstyle, usually used to describe a fancy style

crown rounded part of a hat; also circlet, usually made of precious metal, worn by monarchs

felt compacted cloth, made from wool, fur, or hair, compressed in hot, damp conditions

fillet decorative lace hairnet worn by ladies in the 1400s to contain long hair

five-point bob short style invented by Vidal Sassoon in 1964. The hair was cut into points on both sides of the ears and at the nape of the neck.

hennin type of steeple-hat; a tall, conical hat with a floaty veil, worn by medieval ladies

milliner hatmaker

millinery hats, or the materials needed to make hats

plush extremely soft silk or, sometimes, cotton, where the surface has been brushed so that small fibers stand up, as they do on velvet

pomade greasy substance used in styling hair

tip top part of a hat's crown

wimple lady's veil that is folded to frame the face. Fashionable during the Middle Ages, it is also part of a nun's traditional dress (habit). Many nuns today no longer wear habits or wimples.

Index